MW01231458

So, You *Say* You're a Christian...

Melanie Blievernicht

Ideas into Books® W E S T V I E W
Kingston Springs, Tennessee

Ideas into Books®
W E S T V I E W
P.O. Box 605
Kingston Springs, TN 37082
www.publishedbywestview.com

Copyright © 2023 M Blievernicht LLC
All rights reserved, including the right to reproduction, storage, transmittal, or retrieval, in whole or in part in any form.

ISBN 978-1-62880-261-0

First edition, March 2023

Photo credits:

The author gratefully acknowledges permission to reprint common domain scriptural references from the New King James version of the Bible.

Good faith efforts have been made to trace copyrights on materials included in this publication. If any copyrighted material has been included without permission and due acknowledgment, proper credit will be inserted in future printings after notice has been received.

Digitally printed worldwide by Ingram Spark on acid free paper.

DEDICATIONS

In honor of my Lord Jesus Christ,

Thank You

for your faithfulness and selflessness.

And for my parents,

who showed me how to love the Lord, love people

and do my best to embrace others' and my own

struggles, flaws, or unkindness

with compassion, encouragement, and forgiveness.

You have blessed my life in so many ways!

ACKNOWLEDGEMENTS

Thank You, Lord, for entrusting a third project to me! I am grateful for the opportunity to serve You in whatever form You put on my heart. I pray that this work is more of You, less of me, and is pleasing in Your sight. I praise You for giving me eyes to see, ears to hear, and the courage to speak, so that my time here is not wasted but will return to You fruitful and to the glory of Your kingdom.

Mom & Dad—You are awesome prayer warriors, and I am glad that God chose you to be my parents! Thank you for your wisdom, unconditional love, and support through the rollercoaster ride known as my life. Your presence has multiplied the joy and divided the sorrow. Your kindness and encouragement continue to bless my world!

To my family—You are each such a gift, even though we haven't been able to spend as much time together as we once did. Marriages, kids, jobs, moves, and a pandemic have kept our schedules hopping! I hope that you remember how much I care for you, and I pray that, amidst the world's craziness, you will find God's purpose in your lives.

To Cynthia W., Connie M., Lisa Y., Blake & Lynnette, David T., Steve B., Andrea R., CJ, Kristen, Suellen & Mark, Kimberly and Michael, Linda I., Mary & Dan, Patty S., Kathy T., Joe D., Lisa D., Paula and Sam, Mary P., Jay & Eddie, Pat and Richard D., Joe S., Gary W., Libby L. and Dr. T.—Thank you for helping me weather the last fifteen years of trials and continue to find the divine silver linings on my faith walk. I appreciate your prayers, TLC, and godly counsel. You have been a comfort to my soul.

To my workplace Brothers and Sisters in Christ during these many years, thank you for your amazing hearts for God and the kindness you have shown me. I am privileged to have listened to your testimonies, walked beside you through your hardships, and received your prayers. I am grateful that the Lord surrounded me with such phenomenal people in my home away from home. I pray that He will show you ongoing favor in your own journeys of faith and in those whose lives you touch.

To my EPC and JCA families, thank you for your passion for prayer and ministry, for shining Christ's light brightly, and for making differences in the lives of many people, including mine.

To MC and the rest of the team, thank you for helping me bring this work into existence with your meticulous eyes, creative minds, and big hearts. Your skills and talents are deeply valued and appreciated. Knowing you are part of my team on this journey has brought me peace in the midst of the storm. Here's to #3! Wahoo!

CONTENTS

INTRODUCTION

God calls me to write. I never planned it, nor did I want it or pray for it. But He has been clear in the asking and has been faithful delivering His messages through me. "How do you know it's God and not you?" you might wonder.

Well, for one thing, His requests don't come at times that are convenient or conducive to diving into expensive, emotionally intense, time-consuming projects. Also, I didn't grow up having a dream to one day write a book, much less book(s) that necessitate my own transparency…exposing my own failure, pain, and the messy parts of my life. In addition, when it's time to write, the concepts just flow out of me without brainstorming, outlining, or any prewriting required. I compose entire chapters at a time. My energy level and mood do not impact my ability to put these thoughts onto paper. When I set aside time and pray over the endeavor, God consistently delivers…even when the brain and body should be too tired to produce anything of genuine depth or quality. Lastly, this is the third book which the Lord has called me to write. How does one go from never-wanted-to-write-a-book mode to this-is-the-third-book reality? By God's request, that's how. I have tried to be obedient to His calling, so I cannot duck or dodge His spiritual beckoning through my pen!

So, You Say You're a Christian… stands apart from the other two books. The first, *Walking Faith Forward: Perspectives of Ordinary Life Transformed by Faith*, was a weekly devotional that focused on my personal spiritual growth and perspective of my relationship with God. *Divorce Is Only Human: My Journey with God through Divorce* was my second work. It dealt with my struggle and suffering through a divorce with the Lord as my faithful and true Husband, carrying me through the pain of a broken marriage. Its message was one of encouragement and hope found on the other side of the misery and destruction of my seventeen years of devotion to my husband and the lost dreams attached to our failed relationship.

Which brings me to the here and now. As much as I have prayed for a hope-filled, peace-bringing, tender and loving context of God's will for these chapters, the answer I continue to receive is three-fold:

1. This book is directed to Christians (not for nonbelievers) and is not to be a touchy-feely message.

2. Its purpose is to convey the harsh reality that many Christians may be self-labeled as people of faith, but they are, in fact, consistently weakening their relationship with God through intentionally or unintentionally embracing sin and diminishing the enormity of Jesus' sacrifice, thereby putting the status of their personal salvation in jeopardy.

3. Time is running out.

So, the premise of this text is simple. For those who have a strong relationship with the Lord and who are walking in His statutes, this book will reaffirm their faith and the fruit that their lives are bearing while hopefully give them food for thought. For individuals who believe they are followers of Christ but whose casual and repetitive sinful thoughts, words and actions do not align with His teachings, this work may be the final alarm you are given to reconsider your choices and how they will be judged by our Savior.

This book is not designed to ease your worries. Quite to the contrary, it may make you extremely uncomfortable. God corrects those whom He loves (including me), and I get the distinct impression that—while we have been offered the unconditional love and blessings of God's kingdom—right now we should be concerned about the overwhelming prevalence of intentional sin and how our hypocrisy distances us from the Lord. Saying we love Him and follow His Word, then behaving however we please, does not reflect devotion that should naturally flow from Christians. *God is here*, but are we truly with Him, choosing Him over all else? Or are we too busy worshipping the world's offerings while turning our backs on Jesus, the only Way to salvation?

Tick, tock, tick, tock….

Stress Fixation

Stress seems to find us, no matter how much faith we have. Doctors regularly tell us that one of the reasons we don't feel well is because of our stress level. They prescribe that we need to increase our exercise, sleep more, eat better, bump up our water intake and find hobbies that help us relax. But regardless of however many of these steps we follow, stress still seems to stalk us. Some of our stressors come from simply living in a fallen universe, but we also have to be aware of the devil's mission to destroy our relationship with our Maker and how he loves to further complicate our daily walk.

When we close our eyes at bedtime, stress' eyes are staring back at us. From somewhere we hear the dramatic reminders of the day's, week's, month's (or longer) events that went wrong or need to be addressed. This voice also reminds of us of how helpless we are to manage the things that are completely beyond our control and follows that thought with recalling times in our history when everything went wrong or when we failed. Then, there are variations of "what-if" worst-case scenarios that parade across our imaginations, taunting us with potential crises that could make our already stressful existence even heavier. Our hearts begin to pound when we are supposed to be physically and mentally quieting down. Oftentimes, when we do sleep, it is restless or full of dreams that keep us from feeling restored and refreshed when we wake. And as soon as our eyes pop open, the stress is waiting again, ready to pounce on us with the deluge of panic-inducing thoughts for the day.

It's not only the presence of stress that makes our lives more difficult; it is that we often become so focused on trying to cope with it that we lose sight of God. This isn't intentional. Being overwhelmed with the circumstances we face in this broken world and having to cope with our pain and challenges—as well as the stress that people we care about are going through—is normal. Secular belief centers on man's self-sufficiency to handle all problems, but this perspective promotes the idea that we are alone in the battle. This is not the truth. God is always with those who love Him, and He is ready to help us fight back or fight back on our behalf. Faith is not an innate human experience, nor is the Lord's grace something we can create or consciously apply to our situations. We require God's supernatural intervention at His discretion to aid us in our efforts to stay focused on Him and not allow our stress to pre-occupy our attention.

Are there tasks that must be completed each day? Yes. Do we have to face hurdles that real life gives us, like illness, injury, personality conflicts, workplace demands, family dynamics and other mountains to be climbed? Yes. Can we get tired, depressed, frustrated, and impatient with the lack of sensitivity the world has for our struggles? Yes. Do we obsess over making plans in order to try to control our reality? Yes. Do we find it harder to keep our emotions steady and proportionate when responding to our circumstances? Yes. However, if we are truly keeping God at the center of our lives, we will use these crazy conditions to reinforce how much we depend on Him to be the calm in our storms. We must cling to His promises and the confidence He tells us to have during the trials that find us. Even if all we can do is close our eyes and picture sitting on His knee and telling Him how scared, intimidated, hysterical or unequipped we feel, then just do it. Let His Sovereignty be the tranquility at the center of your chaos. He is the only true Peace we will have in this world, and we have to trust His presence regardless of how hopeless we feel or how miserable and stressed out our minds and bodies are.

Stress has become an idol by default. We have become so consumed by it that its noise shuts out almost everything else. Find the strength that the Lord has given you to persevere. Pray first, then plan. Get into His Word and read His proclamations about the importance of seeking Him above all else. Find a verse that brings you comfort and memorize it to repeat during your day when you feel anxiety building. Let go of your need to control everything and anticipate the Lord making a way for you to move through each demanding season in your life. Refuse to let stress impact your faith and the relationship you have with Jesus. He has overcome the world, and we need to be careful that we are not worshipping stress by giving it all our time. He is the only One worthy of that much attention.

Proverbs 19:21 ❧ Isaiah 30:21

Jeremiah 33:3 ❧ Matthew 6:34

John 14:27 ❧ Proverbs 28:26 ❧ 1 Peter 5:6-7

THE WALK

In terms of what you believe, being a Christian is much deeper than a mere label. It becomes the composition of your heart, mind and soul…transforming your DNA into something beyond the science of organic chemistry, rooted in the very breath of God. I am referring to those who have genuine kinship with the Lord through ownership of their sins, repentance for their wrongdoings, and ultimate humility and gratitude before Christ for all that He has done to save the world through His gift of eternal salvation. He offers a relationship, not a religion. This path is not for the fainthearted, those seeking a life of self-entitlement and self-indulgence, people who expect a trouble-free journey, or individuals who believe that Jesus died to give them a "free pass" from the consequences of their decisions.

For years I have been concerned about the hypocrisy within the church body, at least by those who claim to be part of Christ's family but do not live the walk. These individuals talk a good game but have created their own ideas/definitions/explanations as to who God is/what He thinks/feels/expects outside of His Word. They have also elevated man's role and authority within the church beyond what God has defined it to be. My hope is that we (believers) will take genuine ownership of our relationship with Christ beyond giving it simple lip service and token visits to church on Sundays.

The topics within these chapters may be sensitive and push emotional buttons, but someone needs to speak out to advocate for Christians who may be deceiving themselves. I, myself, am trying to finish the race and keep the faith during a time when the world is shutting God out at every turn, and I don't want to see my brothers and sisters in Christ lose courage or focus on our mission.

Are we stretching our heart muscles and mind on behalf of God's kingdom, or have we checked the "I believe in Jesus" box and are now simply on cruise control for the rest of the ride? Do we only embrace the teachings that are convenient and align with our preferences, or are we seeking His will over our own? It is no coincidence that we are alive here and now as we approach the end of the age. Don't disengage while the Human Race continues to tumble downward and spiral out of control. We are the Lord's front line, if we *choose* to be.

If you are reading this book, don't you know that the Lord has *called you* for such a time as this?

Matthew 23:23-35 ❦ Revelation 15-21 ❦ Esther 4:14

Matthew 7:18-23 ❦ John 4:18-21

Luke 20:46-47 ❦ James 1:22-27 ❦ Isaiah 43:10-13

Psalm 32:8 ❦ 2 Chronicles 7:14-22

TESTIMONY UP!

In the Book of Revelation, the Lord speaks of the faithful and how they are able to overcome the devil and experience salvation "by the blood of the Lamb [Christ's sacrifice] and the word of their [yours and my] testimony." Many Christians are passionate about their faith, yet some are hesitant to talk about Jesus outside the circle of their fellow believers. They claim that their faith and relationship with God is private and intimate, and they aren't comfortable discussing it with others.

News flash! According to God's mission for us, we are supposed to do exactly that! We are His witnesses, vessels to spread the Gospel throughout the world, so we cannot simply take a "pass" because talking about what God has done for us makes us feel awkward. How do you think *He* felt being able to see and experience beforehand and firsthand the false accusations, pain, mocking, suffering, abandonment, torture, and death by suffocation that created the opportunity of salvation for every person who ever lived? Consider the traumatic and lethal experiences of the Apostles as they ventured to distant lands to stand in harm's way while sharing Jesus with the world. Faith isn't about remaining in whatever cocoon of coziness and safety we have wrapped around ourselves. It's about being available to the Lord and fulfilling His will above our own.

This aspect of my daily walk can be a challenge. In the back of my mind, I have lingering thoughts about how someone may react to what I say. However, I have to overcome those concerns and push forward with sharing my faith. One of the easiest lead-ins (for me) to talking about God is praising Him in a simple way. Sometimes, He prompts my memory regarding an item I'm missing at the store checkout in time to run back and retrieve it.

Upon my return to the line, I often say (enthusiastically), "Thank You, Lord, for reminding me about this before I left the store!" Others behind the register or in line may smile, nod and agree or turn away at the statement, but the situation gives me the opportunity to follow up my comment with more genuine affection along the lines of "I'm so grateful for God's love and support in my life." Even if I don't have the appropriate surroundings or time for a deep dive into how Jesus has impacted me, planting seeds of faith through what I say, or my actions can make an impression on a bystander and bloom into curiosity or a possible conversation.

Another significant aspect of my testimony process has come through encounters with people who bristle in anger about faith practices/beliefs in general or towards God specifically (usually related to pain they've experienced). My initial response comes simply from choosing not to leave to avoid a scene. I've not always stayed to continue the conversation, but I am getting better at it. Being willing to bear the brunt of a person's strong emotion or attacks in order to share Jesus with them is uncomfortable. We have to be able to get past the behavior and consider the pain and perspective that are causing it.

I try to listen quietly and carefully, making mental notes of where we share common ground. They may talk about their suffering, to which I attempt to relate and offer support. Sometimes, all I can offer is a non-judgmental ear, my full attention or acknowledging what they are going through with compassion and respect. When I am able, I attempt to weave into our chat times when the Lord has given me strength and hope through my trials. However, even if I never mention the name of Jesus, the love with which I try to handle the situation may speak louder than any personal anecdote I could share with the individual. That, in itself, could set the encounter apart in their mind as being different than they expected…and might leave them wondering why it was so unique…and thinking more about the faith that I follow, and the man known as Jesus.

It reminds me of a conversation my Mom once had with her Dad (my Grandpop). He was a prominent cardio-thoracic surgeon who loved his patients and had been known to cry regarding their medical conditions and suffering. As a young nurse in training, my Mom had heard him criticized by a younger doctor for being too sensitive, emotional and personal with his patients. When she shared what she'd heard with her Dad, he asked about the man's age and nodded with comprehension. He calmly responded, "Honey, he's clearly not old enough or experienced enough yet to understand that sometimes all you can give a patient is a piece of yourself."

I believe that the same holds true for how we, as believers, should treat everyone. The most valuable piece we have to share of ourselves is God's loving presence within us.

So, people of faith, are we willing to step up and share how God has blessed us? Saved us? Provided for us? Delivered us through trials? Healed us? Protected us? Given us strength and hope? Worked miracles in our lives? I am not saying that we must all take to the street corners of the world to shout out dramatic stories of earth-shattering impact. However, God *does* expect us to meet people where they are and offer them accounts of how He has moved on our behalf in various ways, all the while reflecting His love and compassion through our words and actions. To shy away from engaging others with "God talk," or even simple stories of faith, is to deny the sacred nature of our relationship with the Lord.

How much more excited and enthusiastic should we be about the Provider of our eternal salvation than we are about our relatives and friends, careers, hobbies, and favorite sports teams? We need to stop allowing our passion for people, pets and pastimes outrank our eagerness to share how the Lord has moved in our lives! Let's stop making excuses and summon the courage to testimony up!

Revelation 12:10-11 ❧ 1 John 5:9-12 ❧ John 3:31-34

Psalm 96:1-3 ❧ Romans 1:15-20, 10:11-17

1 Peter 3:15-17 ❧ Hebrews 11:1

ULTIMATE AUTHORITY

The world espouses that power can be acquired through birthright, beauty, talent, threat, murder, manipulation, and other means. The coveted lust for power encourages the seeker no matter who or what gets hurt in the mission to capture it. People's twisted and perverted sense of entitlement has become more grossly displayed with the age of the internet, and its captivated audience waits eagerly to be fed and entertained by whatever is available, whether true or not. Sadly, the more technology we create, the less individuals seem to think for themselves when it comes to choosing who gets their attention, time, criticism, or endorsement and/or financial support.

Juxtapose this complete dysfunction and out-of-balance existence with the Lord's instruction in the Word. He offers His grace to give us power to persevere through difficulties. He emphasizes that when we are weak, He is strong, and will be our Advocate and fight spiritual battles on our behalf. God teaches us to embrace our hardships, infirmities, frailties and inadequacies because those human challenges and hurdles bring us closer to Him. They provide opportunities for the world to see His glory through our trials and testimony. Christians also understand that our successes and blessings do not originate with us but with our sovereign Father. We can achieve nothing of value on our own, but the Lord reassures us that we can do all things through Jesus.

Repeatedly, God teaches and reminds us to beware the arrogance of taking credit for His generosity and favor. The world may emphasize self-sufficiency and a do-whatever-it-takes attitude as all you need to make it to the top, but believing this strategy and perspective as truth is idolatry. To think we are the be-all-to-end-all, consummate authority, leader, entertainer, educator, inventor or anything else of our own accord is elevating man above God, and He will allow us to dig our own eternal, pain-filled grave. The Lord has given His own holy Child so that the world could become His sanctified kin and a sin-free bride for His Son. This relationship comes with the comforting blanket of His compassion wrapped in unlimited might. The more we decrease in terms of our own self-importance, while increasing in our awe of and humility before Him, the greater the flow of His ultimate power through our lives.

We need to be careful how much of our relationship with the Lord is the "us" part instead of the "Him." He should always be the majority! If this idea bothers you, I suggest taking some time to examine your heart and weed out the thoughts that center on you. Make a concerted effort to dwell on thoughts that focus on Him. Pray for the will to fight the natural tendency to choose self over Creator. Our world teaches just the opposite and will push into your mind at every chance to crowd out awareness of His true preciousness. We will never be complete or at peace without God's presence at the core of our lives, because of the simple fact that He designed us to one day be with Him and be fulfilled by Him in every way. For those that never except Christ as His Son and Giver of salvation, they will always have emptiness that cannot be filled and longing that will never be explained. No shortcut, substitute, quick fix or workaround exists in lieu of His design. We need to concentrate on worshiping His perfect omnipotence instead of being distracted by the world's illusion and allure of power. We will never have any innate power, other than what God chooses to give us, for the simple reason that we are created beings. His ultimate power moves through us (Christians) but is not of us, and we are blessed to experience the

Holy Spirit in this way. Man's idea of power will never come close to the Lord's.

For example, think about people who consider themselves to be powerful. They may hold elevated positions, yet they can't make anything grow. These individuals can plant a seed, water it, give it sunlight and ideal temperature conditions but cannot consciously "will" anything to develop (though I'm sure some are happy to take credit for a successful harvest). Man does not possess the ability to create anything from nothing (though he can use his creativity to combine elements that God provides, like through artwork), but what a simple thing growing is for the Lord!

Christians need to remain humble before God and honor Him for the power that only He possesses, and we do that by respecting our limits and reminding ourselves that He has a unique purpose for each one of us and has equipped us accordingly. We also need to safeguard against letting our egos override His plans for us. His power is the only one that counts, and He is faithful to His children. So, let us celebrate His ultimate authority and be thankful that it is His—and not ours—to wield.

Jeremiah 10:12-16 ❧ 1 Corinthians 1:18-19

Daniel 3:14-28, 6:4-28 ❧ Matthew 8:2-17, 15:30-31

Mark 4:36-41 ❧ Isaiah 40:10-31 ❧ Exodus 14:10-31

THE STILL, SMALL VOICE

The Bible records conversations that our almighty God had with men, but the Word does not mention that He ranted, raved, yelled, whined, mimicked, mocked, complained or was sarcastic in these interactions. (Yes, Jesus became angered and overturned the money changers' tables in the temple when responding to their disrespect of His Father's house, but His righteous judgment of the situation was quick, truthful and appropriate.) Overall, the Lord communicates much more maturely, effectively and gently than man does, since He understands what we need to know and how best to deliver that information. I guess those other traits are reserved for humans, since we are the ones who have challenges controlling our emotions and behavior. Nothing surprises God, so He doesn't react to things that happen, since He already sees the sum of eternity's events before they've occurred.

Yet, with all that power, He tells us to seek Him in quiet places away from others, where the world can be shut out, and we can share with Him our deepest thoughts and feelings in peace, stillness and isolation from distraction.

The Lord wants to have meaningful dialogue with us, an intimate exchange of time, space, and affection, uninterrupted by the spiritual clutter and unchecked busyness of our daily lives. He faithfully waits for us to carve out these periods of blessings and grace; He enjoys engaging us deeply within our spirits, sometimes so profoundly that we cannot fully explain to another person (especially a nonbeliever) exactly how the process feels or the emotional impact it has on our person.

Spending time with the Lord expands our being in many ways, the most important of which draws us closer to Him. The vision we have of God in our imaginations is a far cry compared to when we will one day stand before Him in His true heavenly form. As we focus more on seeking Him through prayer and listening for His guidance, He reveals more of Himself to us. When we one day enter our heavenly home, it will be familiar because of our relationship with our Father. Our souls will elate in returning to the One who masterfully designed us, breathed life into our bodies and for Whom we have longed during our lives on Earth. His voice will have the same warm and loving tones that He had with Adam and Eve, Abraham, Moses, Noah, David and His other servants throughout history. His presence will fill us completely.

Perhaps we would learn more from the Lord if we kept our mouths closed and our spirits open and available to consider His thoughts, ponder His ways, and receive His direction for our lives. We all want others to listen to what we have to say, and the Lord expects no less. He wants us to develop spiritually, which we can only experience with His help, and He was kind enough to write down His many bits of wisdom, instructions, and commandments to help us remember.

So, if we Christians are frustrated by not "hearing from God" regarding our prayers, questions and requests, please consider whether we are making ourselves available to hear His loving responses. Are we asking Him to yell over the loud chaos in our lives instead of listening for His still, small voice during quiet periods set aside for just the two of us? Are we giving Him the sacrifice of our time and attention without constantly asking for and expecting Him to deliver our wish list each day? Are we available and truly interested in what He has to tell us? If we *have* heard from Him, are we being obedient to His voice and wisdom and taking His words to heart?

1 Kings 19:9-11 ❧ John 8:43-47 ❧ Hebrews 2:1-4, 3:7-12

John 10:1-5, 16 ❧ Revelation 3:19-22

The Color of Truth

Each of us is unique. Although billions of people have walked the earth, no person is a duplicate of someone else. Even identical twins have differences, though they may not be obvious in passing. God celebrates the variety of individuals He has sown across the world, from their personalities and gifts to the color of their skin and sound of their voices. He loves and blesses all His children, even those who have animosity towards Him or who choose not to be in a relationship with Him. His capacity for unconditional love translates into a desire that all His children be saved…even those who perpetuate pain, destruction and suffering.

Jesus perfectly modeled how to treat others. He did not ignore, mistreat or target anyone who came from other places and ways of life. His love enveloped people whose skin color, sex, body type, age, language, abilities, upbringing, beliefsor socioeconomic status was different than His. Those who were neglected and ostracized by society were blessed with His compassion and gentleness. Even tyrants and criminals were given the offer of salvation. He came to sacrifice His life for all of us, no matter how sinful our behavior.

Today, racism runs rampant in this country. This is nothing new since the practice has been around for thousands of years. Long ago, groups adopted a manufactured ideology of elitism that somehow elevated those who deemed themselves to be more valuable than others based on their skin color. This is a blatant sin and goes against the Lord's teaching. However, its popularity and acceptance grew because people enjoyed the idea of possessing a higher status in whatever form they perceived it to exist. That sense of entitlement has gotten worse over the years, and our society and world continue to battle this toxic presence in our midst. Many, consciously or unconsciously, have used it as an excuse to avoid social interactions, supporting those in need in their local communities or becoming engaged with the crises that citizens in the international community face.

We are now at the point where large populations in our nation wish to make our racist history completely disappear. They believe that by destroying evidence of its existence and refusing to acknowledge the catastrophic harm that has been done to people of color, they may continue to live without racism being a personal concern or inconveniently impacting their lives. They are not interested in working towards equality for those upon whom others have and will continue to tread but instead promoting the destruction of those who believe in that equality, speaking the truth and stopping the oppression.

Why is it so difficult to defeat this ignorant, anti-Christian perspective? I think one reason is that racism is taught within families through word and action. Hating those who aren't like us becomes a right that elders encourage and demonstrate for their children. Those youth are praised—and often rewarded—for mimicking these behaviors, adopting this sinful philosophy and taking pleasure in exercising their "power" over those not like them. Surrounding oneself with likeminded individuals exacerbates the evil, because there are no voices speaking God's truth of how we are supposed to treat one another. Furthermore, a "we-versus-them" mentality, as if an enemy is already lining up to threaten one's way of life, is created and reinforced from a very early age.

Fear also contributes to this cancerous mindset. People fear personal characteristics that are different from their own.But instead of reaching out to learn more about individuals whose paths or experiences contrast ours, many individuals distance themselves from these simple opportunities for conversation because they are uncomfortable. Lacking the courage to, or interest in, wanting to find out more about others and confront our fear can create passive racism which is still oppressive. Our culture frequently seems to focus on distancing versus finding common ground when it comes to broadening our relationships beyond familiar groups.

Another aspect to consider is that our society and media has enabled everyone to become a victim (without cause) of something or someone. So, racism is a default being used to blame others for our own poor decisions, mistakes or a way to take out our frustrations on people we consider to be easy targets. Racism has become an acceptable substitution for personal accountability instead of taking ownership for our words and actions (or lack thereof).

History has recorded—and continues to record—the abuse, exclusion and discrimination of individuals based on their skin color for these reasons and more. A significant number of these incidents were and are committed by people who claim to be Christians, whether they are actively oppressing others at work, in public places, on social media or in their homes. These "Christian" individuals are deceiving themselves! Their nasty thoughts, words and actions perpetuate malice and intentionally injure others. God clearly states that we are to love Him and then love others *as we do ourselves*. For those who continue to malign persons whose skin color is not their own, they are reveling in the sin of racism…period. It doesn't matter how many people do it or by what justification they try to excuse it. Hate is hate, and the Lord does not condone this behavior in any form.

People of God, we need to bring our hearts before Him and ask that He cleanse us of any unrighteous attitudes or perceptions regarding others' skin color or any characteristic they have that we think or feel creates physical and emotional distance between us as human beings. Request of Him that He give us courage to act against such demonstrations by others—that we not continue to be complacent with the racism happening around us. Let us extend the Lord's love to everyone in a way that, if all of us were blind, we wouldn't be able to distinguish anything other than kindness and compassion from our fellow man. In Revelation, God's throne is surrounded by people of all colors, from all nations and speaking all languages.

If we stay on this course of self-worship through the idolatry of racism, we may find that we no longer have a place before His throne. Repentance is required as part of salvation, so we cannot passionately love to hate others and still expect to have a room reserved in our Father's house in heaven.

Revelation 7:9-10 ❧ Galatians 3:28 ❧ Acts 17:26

John 13:34 ❧ James 2:1-10 ❧ Matthew 7:12 ❧ 1 John 2:9

Psalm 52:1-7 ❧ Ephesians 2:10 ❧ Psalm 139:13-16

ABOUT BAPTISM

Christians are very familiar with the concept of baptism. Put simply, it is an outward demonstration or display of a person's spiritual rebirth through their faith in Jesus Christ. Before Jesus formally began His ministry, He asked His cousin, John the Baptist, to baptize Him. Although resistant at first, John finally agreed. After John finished the process, the sky opened, and the Father spoke, announcing His relationship to His Son and how pleased He was with Him. Jesus didn't need to be baptized for forgiveness of sin, since He was already without sin or imperfection. He requested John's assistance to fulfill His Father's will of anointing Him with the Holy Spirit and to show mankind that baptism is an acknowledgment of faith.

Fast forward almost two thousand years, and we find that man has inserted all sorts of rules about the baptismal process. For instance, some Christians claim that you are not truly saved unless you've been baptized. This statement is not scripturally accurate. A believer is saved the moment they genuinely accept Christ as their Savior and repent of their sins. The most obvious person who was granted salvation without baptism was Dismas, the thief hanging to the right of Jesus at Calvary. His pronouncing that Jesus was without sin and didn't deserve the criminals' punishment, as well as begging Jesus to remember him (once Christ had ascended into heaven), demonstrated his faith in the Son of God and his repentance for the wrong he had done in his life. There was no time for a water baptism, but our Lord lovingly responded to him that he would be in paradise with Christ that very day. This is the amazing grace that only our God can give, grace that sees the heart's intent, first and foremost, versus all our sin and collective spiritual garbage.

Then, there are some Christians who instill fear in parents by claiming that God will not welcome babies or children into heaven unless they've been baptized. This false teaching is wrong for several reasons. First, there is no such instruction about children in the Bible. Second, Jesus told His followers to let the children "come unto me" and that the enthusiasm and innocence of youth are qualities that adults should have about the idea of heaven. Third, baptism was created as a symbol primarily for adults who want to publicly acknowledge that they have been "born again," and who are excited about the new life Christ has given them. Being cognizant of one's sins, taking ownership of them and repenting for them are key elements of spiritual rebirth. Although some youth grasp these concepts and desire to be baptized, the majority of those exploring and developing their faith are not children, and certainly not infants.

In addition, there are believers who insist that only individuals baptized in their denomination or in their tank, lake, ocean locale, etc., or using their script and blessings or having taken all their classes on salvation are actually saved. The Bible debunks this as well. The Holy Spirit is more than capable of baptizing those seeking Christ without the plethora of rules and guidelines that many churches have manufactured. He is reaching the hearts and minds of people across the globe who may never have the opportunity for baptism, but who are saved nonetheless. Man has created baptismal requirements that God never stated or implied in His Word.

The bottom line is that Christ's example was simply that. He didn't establish baptism as a pass-or-fail requirement for salvation but as a symbolic way to show the world we have been given new life. He did not frame the baptism experience with a bunch of rules and rituals; man did that to try and assume authority that belongs only to Jesus.

We, as individuals and members of God's church body, need to be careful about spreading misinformation about the Lord's intent and qualifications for salvation that do not line up with scripture, because we will be held accountable for bolstering falsehoods and intentionally misleading others. The Lord is not interested in man's efforts to perpetuate elitism when it comes to the path to salvation, and we will be made to answer for interfering with His edicts.

Matthew 3:11-17, 18:1-6 ❧ Mark 10:13-16

Acts 2:37-41 ❧ Acts 8:26-40

CHRISTIANS ARE NOT IMMUNE

Contrary to popular belief, Christians do not lead easier or more privileged lives than secular individuals. If fact, quite the opposite is often true. If someone chooses not to have a relationship with Jesus—or even entertain the notion of His status as the Son of God and Provider of Salvation—then the devil has no reason to target them at a spiritual level. Man has already done the work for him, by worshipping something or someone other than the Lord. So, those souls are already on the path to eternal suffering outside the presence of God. Mission accomplished! However, the Lord's family members are moving targets whom the enemy sets out to deceive, destroy and kill. Our worship and devotion to the one, true God drives the devil crazy, since his only obsession is lusting for that very worship and devotion above everything else. To BE God is his sole motive for his delusional and malicious actions.

He will do anything and everything in his power to turn us away from our Creator. People from every walk are subject to his attempts at manipulation and abuse, whether he uses their circumstances, health and emotions, egos, vanity, pride, sin, or natural events to twist believers' lives into stress-filled journeys. The enemy hopes to make us question our faith and belief in the Trinity. Though not all our personal challenges are intentionally inflicted by the devil (some result from our fallen world), he twists and perverts many situations into layers of painful experiences that clutter our minds and take focus away from Jesus. We are only human, so our attention and energy can be easily distracted or divided, thereby impacting time we could be spending communing with Him. Regardless of the hurdles in our path, our confidence lies in knowing that God supplies us with whatever we need to persevere through the trials ahead.

In His Word the Lord also warns believers about how spiritual and physical dynamics will change at the end of the age, and this shift is well under way. Some self-proclaimed "Christians" have clearly redefined their beliefs which no longer align with the holy scriptures. Their behavior reveals shades of darkness at an ever-increasing rate, whether through blatant rejection of Christ's teaching, or apathy towards what they once held to be sacred. Many appear unaware that they are actively distancing themselves from God and have lost the ability to objectively examine their own actions—nor are they interested in doing so. Some of them seem to have become polarized within society, having either surrounded themselves with individuals who support and encourage their counter-Christian ideas and philosophies, or by having withdrawn into their personal microcosm of reality and disengaging from faith- and fellowship-based activities altogether.

The Bible boldly states love will grow cold during the end of the age; man will seek after his sinful desires and wrap himself in thoughts and pastimes that are self-worshiping, self-gratifying, self-destructive and faith-abolishing. The news is presently full of stories that center on individuals who think they are gods. Many have proven that no amount of common sense, prevalence of morals or numerous laws will stop their rampages and tearing down of what the Lord created for good. They desire nothing more than to have unlimited power with the world at their mercy. Sound familiar? It should. They are doing the devil's dirty deeds for him, and the worst part is they enjoy it…not concerned with the ramifications and ultimate eternal torture that awaits them when this mortal life is over.

Do not fall asleep or become complacent, my friends! Spiritual warfare has been a reality since the devil was kicked out of heaven, and God warns us to stay alert and vigilant while clinging to His promises. We are not immune to the devil's poisonous and deadly strategies, since our free will allows us options that lead away from Jesus.

The Lord tells us the path to salvation is narrow, and—unlike today's wolves in sheep's clothing promoting many paths to heaven—He is not kidding. Jesus will turn His back on some "Christian" posers on Judgment Day, and you need to be clear about your loyalties before He returns. Believing in Christ will always come with a cost, whether it is the sacrifice of our time, resources or experiencing persecution, just as His gift came at the highest price.

When the moment arrives, will our lives reflect that we chose Him or ourselves?

1 Corinthians 6:9-10 ❧ 2 Corinthians 10:3-6

Matthew 24:3-14 ❧ Psalm 37:12-16 ❧ 2 Kings 6:15-17

1 Peter 5:8-10 ❧ Isaiah 59:17 ❧ Romans 1:22-32

BEWARE THE POSERS

One of the things that deters people from seeking the Lord is the abundance of individuals who pretend to be Christians in order to reap the benefits that may accompany such a claim or affiliation. These fakers create a distaste in the mouths of those who genuinely want to know more about the Lord. During the early years of my life, I only saw the most dramatic poser "Christians" and opportunists on TV. Yep, they were televangelists, most of whom promised easier lives, healing and prosperity for a donation of a certain amount. Then, about a decade after moving to Atlanta, a friend invited me to a church of his business associate, where I could participate in a social gathering, was introduced to the pastor, and enjoyed their New Year's Eve celebration. Although I appreciated his thoughtfulness of including me, something felt off about the pastor. I tried to look beyond his extremely expensive clothing, heavy jewelry, perfectly manicured appearance and slight strut to discern exactly what bothered me, because I didn't want to assume the cliché about rich spiritual leaders to be true. My next visit the following weekend provided me the clarity I sought.

The service began as I expected with praise and worship music, and some of the congregation appeared to be very engaged. The pastor seemed less genuine than the other attendees in his passion for that part of the service. The next segment was the offering, and he discussed the importance of tithing. Just when I thought he'd done a decent job of encouraging his spiritual family to give back to the Lord, he whipped out a check and began pacing on the stage waving it around and describing how generous he had decided to be with his personal tithe *and* offering that week. I sat their amazed at his self-stroking, prideful presentation. When the collection was complete, his teaching began and was on a topic I'd heard many times. The content didn't move me, but the lesson may have touched the hearts of others.

As I expected him to wrap up, he invited a handful of members and guests (including me) to the front near the raised platform which some people refer to as an altar. I approached from the far-right side of the stage, and he came towards me first. As I stopped to watch him come down the few steps, I noticed a man walking up behind me. I wasn't sure what was going on, but I didn't care for a stranger being at my back and in my personal space. Over the course of a few seconds, I realized that this "pastor" was showboating and wanting to make some sort of demonstration of his "spiritual" power. Quickly, I spoke with the Lord and asked Him to protect me from whatever mockery this man was making in His name and to please root my feet to the floor. I prayed that He, and only He, would control my speech or have me remain silent.

A few seconds later, the pastor spit in my face (I think he had intended to make it look like he was breathing forcefully on me.) then took the palm of his hand and pressed it to my forehead and shoved forcefully, trying to knock me backwards in an apparent display of his "power." That's when I understood why that man was behind me. He was part of the dramatic production, and I imagine that some people got swept up in the excitement and idea of the Holy Spirit moving through them in such a way that they willingly fall back to try to prove how faith-filled they are. Well, the Holy Spirit was definitely there! He kept me anchored to that floor, unflinching, upright and strong, completely clear and confident in defying this man's theatrics without a word but giving him a look of curiosity when his efforts had absolutely no effect on me. When he realized that the game was up, he turned and waived a hand in my face dismissively and said, "Clearly, the Spirit is not with this one." He proceeded down the line of other people who had been invited to the stage. Interestingly enough, very few of them apparently "had" the Spirit. It made me wonder how God's demonstration with my truthful posture had influenced the other people in the line and forced them to consider what this man was trying to sell them.

What amused me the most was that I had just published my first book for the Lord! A book that earned two awards and a book signing at a local Barnes & Noble in Atlanta! That task, alone, was something I would not have been able to accomplish without God's blessing every aspect of it; yet, the leader of this church arrogantly turned his back on me for not glorifying his ego. This man who behaved like a peacock, had his own driver and bodyguard, clearly lived well beyond the average means of his flock, and did everything to elevate himself was far from a man of God. But people followed him.

You would think that this was the end of the story—but wait! There's more! After the service ended, I was invited as a guest to one of the classes they require you to take to join the church. You'll never guess what it was: it was a class on learning how to speak in tongues! I had to take a moment to collect myself before entering the room, because the Bible clearly states that speaking in tongues is a gift given only by the Holy Spirit. My perspective on this church body and leadership sank even lower, when the instructors told the participants to pray, open their mouths and make noises. I am not kidding. They claimed that anyone could learn to speak, but that someone else would have to interpret what was said. I was astonished that people believed this propaganda! You can't manufacture the Holy Spirit! God's not responsible for edifying man's ego! When the facilitator came by my chair, where I was sitting quietly and apologizing to the Lord for this blatant atrocity of a class, she asked if she could help me and encouraged me to make noises. I just sadly shook my head, slowly stood up, told her that I wasn't going to try to fake something that is God's holy gift to be used at His discretion and then walked out.

The shock and disbelief on the faces in the room was priceless, as if I had stopped at each person's chair and slapped them. The instructor didn't know what to say, since I appeared to be the only uncooperative attendee in their years of peddling this scheme. Clearly, this church was not a place founded on truth and respect for the Lord, and I had seen firsthand that good-hearted Christians who are seeking God can still lack common sense, Biblical knowledge, and the fortitude to speak up against the false teachings of the world.

Don't be a sellout to, or enabler of, the show-boaters who are using faith to promote themselves and satisfy their need for money and attention. Seek out healthy church bodies, where the leadership is accountable for their instruction and the teachings come directly from the Bible. Do your own research and study the topics discussed at your church. Don't take anyone's word as truth until you use God's Word as your sounding board. If a church leader is threatened by your questions and concerns about what is being taught instead of being eager to discuss your thoughts and opinions, consider it confirmation that you probably need to find a new church home. Not all Christian spiritual leaders have the humility, self-accountability and profound sense of responsibility that is required for pastoring a congregation. Find a church family that has it, and you will have found a heavenly treasure.

2 Corinthians 11:13-15 ⚜ Matthew 7:15-17 ⚜ 1 Timothy 6:3-5

2 Timothy 3:13 ⚜ Proverbs 16:5, 18 ⚜ Romans 12:3

TRUE STEWARDSHIP

When God created us, He gave us the incredible responsibility of taking care of everything He spoke into being in this world, a duty that started thousands of years ago and continues today.

When church members think of stewardship, they often focus only on their financial commitments to the Kingdom without considering the breadth and depth of what God has left to our oversight.

For instance, the Lord expects us to look out for the plant and animal life, not just in the context of food, personal land/property, and pets, but our community ownership of the earth and animal-kind in our local areas, nation and on this planet. Are we advocating for the land that provides life-giving nutrients via foliage, fruits, vegetables, and nuts? Are we protecting our forests which generate essential oxygen and other provisions through a variety of ecosystems? Are we ensuring that the animal kingdom, whether neighborhood bunnies or endangered species across the globe, is preserved and can thrive as was intended? What about the bodies of water on our planet? Are we insisting that our watersheds and oceans (and the life contained therein) are treated with the utmost respect and preservation? The answer to these questions, for most people, is "No."

More importantly, the Lord has asked us to love and watch over each other—even our enemies. Are we actually embracing His commandment, or does our affection and concern end at the edge of our family-and-friends circle, if it even extends that far? What are we doing to stand against violation of human rights in our states, nation, and the rampant evil oppressing individuals all over the world? How are we lifting up our homeless populations and empowering them to re-engage in society? What steps are we taking to create community mentalities, so that our children and elderly have the nurturing and support they need to thrive? Are we using our resources to supplement and enrich the lives of our veterans, individuals with disabilities, and families that have medical or economic challenges? Are we providing safe places where people suffering from abuse can live until they are able to transition back into their own homes? What supplies and manpower are we sending to other countries to minister to them through God's Word, basic food stores and medical care? Do we offer a kind and empathetic ear to those around us who need emotional support? How are we choosing to spread the unlimited hope, compassion and love that Jesus has given us to share?

We say we are Christians, but is the world seeing the fruit of our beliefs, including being God's generous hands and feet, or do we only adopt the commandments that are comfortable and convenient for us?

Clearly, when you consider the overwhelming scope of blessings that God has set under our purview, it can be difficult to grasp. No one can do everything; however, the Lord has equipped us with the Holy Spirit and each other to form the perfect team for his ministry.

Be encouraged to spread your wings of faith by taking baby steps toward creating or further developing your stewardship capabilities, in addition to financial donations you may make. Find ways to fortify and protect our world through channels that touch your heart. If you love animals, reach out to a rescue organization or sanctuary and volunteer. If you are concerned about pollution and don't already recycle what you can from your garbage, then try to start doing so. If you love spending time in the water, do some research and find out where you can lend a hand to help pick up trash at your local lake or assist organizations that focus on ocean cleanups. If you are concerned about the depletion of our natural resources, take shorter showers, use your own bags at the grocery store, start a blog to increase awareness and action around the issue, or find alternate avenues through which you can help our planet.

As far as opportunities to love people, you don't have to look far to find numerous ways to sow into the welfare of the less fortunate. Due to society's preoccupation with busyness and self-centeredness, many suffering souls have become invisible because their fellow men do not notice or care about their circumstances. *But*, it's not too late to change! Shelters, hospitals, soup kitchens, nursing homes, food banks, schools, and most charitable organizations are always grateful for assistance. Whether you'd enjoy preparing a meal for the homeless, tutoring an (academically) at-risk student after school, assisting a homebound individual with errands or keeping them company, providing a ride for a person who has no transportation, or writing a letter to someone in prison, the needs are many, and the help appreciated. People from all walks of life are hurting and seeking relief from their struggles. Get creative and develop your own unique way to share God's love. Brainstorm with the excitement and passion that children have with a lemonade stand. They aren't thrilled about the lemonade itself but by the potential that selling it represents. What potential drive and ideas do you have to serve your local and global neighbors?

Effective stewardship of God's gifts requires intentional focus and investment of our time, money, prayer and effort. Please examine your priorities and give what you can, however you can, to whomever you can each day. Let's be the army of change that our Father expects us to be!

SO, YOU SAY YOU'RE A CHRISTIAN...

Genesis 1:26-28, 2:15, 19-20 1 Peter 4:8-11

1 Timothy 5:1-8 ❧ Matthew 25:14-30 ❧ Philippians 2:1-4

IF GOD SAYS IT'S HOLY...

I'm not sure how many members of God's family can list most of the Ten Commandments, though these instructions are essential to our spiritual health. Over the years I've come to notice that one of the Lord's commands is often neglected or altogether ignored; it's His fourth decree: "Remember the Sabbath Day, to keep it holy." God distinguished His day of rest—the day He looked back over the six days of His labor and creativity—as a time set apart, or holy, when compared to the other weekdays. Personally, I don't believe that God required a respite because He has infinite energy. However, He knew that His masterpiece, mankind, needed guidance in order to do what would be best for them. If left without instructions, humans would exhaust themselves before maturing in their ability to take healthy down time, particularly time to develop spiritual growth and relationship with the Lord. Why do you think God spelled out the Commandments as He did? We have short memories and vast tendencies to be drawn toward sinful choices, so frequent reminders are necessary.

Consider the Commandments that come before His reference to the Sabbath Day (4th Commandment):

1. I am the Lord thy God. Thou shalt have no other Gods before Me.
2. Thou shalt not make unto thee any graven image.
3. Thou shalt not take the name of the Lord thy God in vain.

So, God's top four rules to help us live our best lives are about our relationship with Him. Just because one of those relates to setting time aside, during which you relax and recharge your batteries away from work and spend time with Him, doesn't make it any less important or powerful in the spiritual realm.

It sounds simple enough, but asking some Christians these days to honor the Sabbath would equate to taking their cell phone away for twelve hours! Respecting this 24-hour period is not about being lazy but intentionally resting, practicing your faith, focusing on God, and lifting up what the Lord says is holy. Think about the physical and spiritual healing and enriching that is possible without the frenzied chaos of our to-do lists pushing and pulling us in every direction.

We pray for peace, but then we make little-to-no room to welcome it into our schedules. We yearn for ways to get ahead without ever considering that being obedient to God's commands is always the most direct path to maximum efficiency, strength, and perseverance. Our tiny human brains are limited by our arrogance and audacity in deciding how, when, where and to what extent we want the Lord to give us His grace. Yet, He has already bestowed on us ten essential laws that will supernaturally draw us closer to Him and His will for our lives. He is available, but we are not; sometimes, not even on His holy day of restoration. Oftentimes, we are the ones who adopt or reject His guidance based on our own logic, plans, and priorities.

So, if you are truly seeking to deepen your faith, embrace His teachings wholeheartedly, even if they appear to conflict with your schedule. He created time, but we are the ones limited by it. Unplug from the world for a day each week and honor Him by resting the body and focusing the heart and mind on who He is. Learn from His example and wise design for us.

Genesis 2:1-3 ❧ Deuteronomy 5:12-15 ❧ Ezekiel 20:19-20

Matthew 12:1-13 ❧ Luke 13:10-17

To Be Content or Not to Be Content

One of the lessons we learn from Scripture is to be content no matter our circumstances. For Christians this edict is fine and dandy when things are going our way. Success at work, check. Relationships going well, check. Good health, check. Financial stability, check. I'm sure the list would be quite impressive, were we to include all aspects of life's major angles. Yet, even when days appear to roll by without conflict or concern, many people still long for more, better, faster or fancier "whatevers." For them, regardless of how amazing or rare their blessings are, there are never enough of them.

Then enters the journey through the challenges that inevitably shake our lives…death of a loved one, loss of a job, end of a relationship, dysfunctional family dynamics, diagnosis of an illness (self, family member, friend), injury from an accident, unexpected financial hardship, and sometimes, these events come in waves that seem impossible to persevere.

Yet Jesus tells us not to lose hope or peace; He has overcome the tribulation in the world and has equipped us, through faith, to get through the storms. Paul shares that he focuses on finding a state of contentment, regardless of the abuse, ostracization and physical hurdles he faces. James instructs us to count the trials we fall into as joy. In short, if we suffer the pain of this fallen world with Christ, we will revel even more in sharing our eternal lives with Him in glory.

I must admit that conquering this particular task has often been elusive for me. I have found myself on my knees and in tears many times, crying out to the Lord with grief, trust, fear and vulnerability. During these struggles, it's difficult to feel victorious in my faith. Sometimes, all I can manage to say is that I will mentally count these experiences as joy, even if my emotions are quite to the contrary. The scripture speaks the truth, so my prayers ask Him to reveal His genuine joy to me. I want to find His blessings in every circumstance, and—no matter what happens—I cling to His promises and wait for their fulfillment.

Do you believe in His words about contentment as well? Do you struggle with being content in your circumstances? Do you have peace with the state of your life, or are you one of those people waiting for the perfect circumstances and for whom enough blessings are never enough?

1 Timothy 6:6-11 ⚜ Philippians 4:11-13 ⚜ Hebrews 13:5-6

Matthew 6:24-33 ⚜ James 4:1-10 ⚜ Psalm 23

WORSHIP AND PRAISE...SORT OF...

If you are reading this book, then you probably already have a solid understanding of God's totally indescribable, unfathomable, unattainable, incomprehensible state of being. There is no scale that we can use to compare ourselves to Him. As a created being, man has limited intelligence and awareness, so his finite experience versus God the Creator's unlimited-ness has no common point of reference except Jesus. The Lord's profound love for us would not leave us alone in the darkness of a fallen world. His Son volunteered to bear the painful and heavy yokes of sin we carry on our backs to protect us when payment would one day be due. He is the reason we celebrate the Father's adoption of us into His kingdom! We—literally, spiritually, and academically—are not capable of saving ourselves from death, so we should be fired up about honoring God with song, prayer, dance, praise and whatever other forms of worship and celebration bring glory to our Rescuer and Redeemer.

Yet, do we express our gratitude to Him for His generosity? Do we cheer for His mercy, patience, and undeserved forgiveness? Do we sing praises to Him and get excited about His affection for us? Are we fired up to be someone who has been given eyes to see and ears to hear the Gospel truth and celebrate our salvation, when most of the world is blind and deaf to it? Do we bow before Him and appreciate the holy gifts we've received, though we did nothing to earn them? Are we amazed and humbled that the One who saw our every freckle and heard our laughter before we were ever conceived adored us even then?

If you genuinely value the privilege of being part of His family, then show Him! Do not go through the motions of praise and worship mechanics for the sake of others who might be watching. Be with Him throughout your day with no witnesses. Whisper kind words of love to Him for His always being with you. Hum Him a song of thanksgiving while you sit on hold during a phone call. Convey your thanks to Him for a fitful night's sleep when you wake the next morning. Praise Him for everyday miracles that bring you joy, whether a "just right" cup of coffee, the antics of a pet anticipating a walk or car ride or getting the closest parking spot during a storm. Daydream of holding His hand, walking beside Him and sharing gratitude regarding the amazing world He designed for us. Speak to Him with a heart of thanksgiving for every blessing that was made possible through Jesus. Ask Him questions in an effort to get to know Him better. Draw closer to Him by spending time basking in who He is.

If we are not excited about the idea of putting off our to-do list to make time for praise and worship, we may want to re-evaluate our faith priorities and figure out exactly what we think our holy Lord deserves. If not praise and worship, then what? How about so very much more than we could ever possibly give?!?!

Hebrews 13:15 ❧ Psalm 150 ❧ 2 Samuel 7:22

Daniel 4:34-37 ❧ John 4:23-24

Revelation 19:9-10 ❧ Psalm 95:1-7

1 Chronicles 16:29-36 ❧ Acts 16:22-26

Man's Blind Spot for Money

Money. It's one of the biggest hot-button topics you will find. People are very sensitive about their finances, whether they are disciplined budgeters and spenders, or are completely lax with their fiscal management. Individuals use various filters when deciding what is a worthy investment: quantity required, amount of risk, value of potential return, overall benefit to self. However, when you combine money talk and God, some folks become extremely emotional, aggressive and/or defensive about their choices. Why is that?

In the Old Testament, God's Word establishes a tithing principle—to donate the first ten percent of the blessings He gives us, whether our earnings, resources, or time, back to Him via His church, other ministries, and our communities. Abraham (Abram, at the time) was the first individual who did this of his own accord with his tithe to the King of Salem, Melchizedek. Melchizedek was a priest who the Bible states had no parents or genealogy, an interesting distinction considering how family lines are emphasized in the Word, and especially with those responsible for serving the Lord. He accepted Abram's tithe and blessed him. Theologians believe that Melchizedek is actually Jesus, since the Bible clearly recognizes Him as someone who is unidentifiable but holding a position of significant spiritual authority.

Another example of this process was when the Israelites, God's chosen people, honored Him by presenting the first fruits of their labor (plants harvested, animals raised, etc.) during designated feast times. God established the importance of acknowledging His provision and building a relationship of trust through tithing. This was a weighty demonstration of faith, even though man was only required to give back a small percentage of what he had been given.

Back to the money issue, we see various references to money and tithing in the Bible, yet many Christians are uncomfortable with the concept. Jesus told the people to "render unto Caesar what is Caesar's and unto God what is God's." Well, God created everything, so technically we should be giving Him everything we have. In addition, His compassion and sacrifice provide us with eternal salvation, on which we cannot possibly put a price. However, the Lord does not demand all our resources and assets; He asks only the first ten percent. What we give above and beyond that is up to us.

For those who understand grace, we know that it is impossible to out-give God. He has already provided for all our needs, but those who honor Him with tithes and offerings understand that being obedient to the Lord ranks above our everyday basic priorities. We also know that He will not abandon us if we are unable to financially tithe. We have other gifts that we can donate to Him, such as our time, prayers, service, and things we own but that would help others more than we need them. He is not focused on the amount but in our honoring His instructions with the right mindset and spirit.

In 2 Corinthians 9:6-9, the Lord tells us that He loves a cheerful giver, so if we aren't excited about the opportunity to give and the positive impact His work is doing, we should refrain from donating altogether. Money given out of obligation and resentment isn't a blessing to God or us. If people are hung up on believing that the money is theirs, no one should tell them how to spend it, and that they can still have a healthy relationship with God without having to rely on His guidance with their finances (putting money matters above faith), they are mistaken. We don't get to decide what is important to the Lord, and if our perspective is us-focused instead of Him-centered, we will miss crucial lessons in our spiritual walk.

Another common criticism of tithing is complaining along the lines of "...you never know where the money goes...." If Christians don't trust their church to use their donations wisely, then find a new church. We can control circumstances around our giving, and God can see our intention to honor Him with our resources. If you don't have a church home, then donate your tithe to an organization you trust that does God's work. There are many groups that do mission work locally, nationally and internationally and whose efforts minister to vulnerable populations across the globe.

Once I was with a friend when we were approached by a homeless man asking for money. She apologized to him by saying she didn't have any cash, but as soon as he walked away, she confessed to having money but not wanting to give it to him because she thought he would use it to buy alcohol. Bible check moment! The Lord does not instruct us to give to the needy only after an exhaustive screening as to how they intend to use the money we give them! It is not for us to judge one's intent but to be God's hands of love. If the needy see condemnation in the eyes of the Lord's family, what hope do we have to offer them the Good News of something better? Why would they listen to us talk about His love for them, compassion, and sacrifice when we are too busy deciding who is worthy or not worthy of our few dollars?

I've heard some individuals claim not to tithe because they say they can't afford it...that every penny goes towards paying the bills. I can speak to this situation very well, because during my divorce I had very little. I was unable to generate the two incomes required to support the bills on the house, so I had to liquidate my retirement fund and went through all my savings. I had my internet, cable and trash service shut off, and my neighbors were kind enough to let me come to their homes to use their internet as well as putting my trash in their cans.

My parents sent me $100 a month for food. I was eating pots of rice and beans supplemented by protein shakes that a friend (who knew I had fallen upon hard times) regularly gave me. I sold furniture to pay for the utilities so that I could keep the house comfortable for potential homebuyers touring my residence month after month. I had no "luxuries," so-to-speak, but I was blessed to have a roof over my head for the 4-5 years it took my house to sell. "What does this have to do with tithing," you ask?

Everything! In my efforts to continue to tithe faithfully during this long period of hardship, I transitioned from financial giving to more time investment. I stepped up my volunteer activities, including helping my church with setting up/breaking down, ushering, serving snacks, childcare and canvasing neighborhoods to spread the word about the church. I reached out to one of my pastors who had phenomenal stories of miracles he'd personally experienced, encouraged him to write a book about his testimony, and began transcribing his notes onto a computer and then proofing/editing the content. During these years I took several people who had no place to live into my home, so that they would be safe during the difficult time of transition in their lives.

And the result? God provided for me and the people in my home! I received His favor through different channels. I had relatives reach out with unsolicited financial gifts that helped me pay bills that backed up. Other loved ones came over to help me with physical projects that my injured back couldn't handle, including help with painting my kitchen, installing a garage door, and ridding my attic of squirrels. Several people contacted me about tutoring their children, which provided income I desperately needed. I called the mortgage company about a letter they sent regarding my escrow account (post-dated for two months later), and they said it was sent because I was a month ahead on my mortgage payments. I spent fifteen minutes trying to explain that their system was wrong because I had only a few dollars in the bank and lived paycheck to paycheck, but the rep politely but firmly insisted I was incorrect and promptly hung up. Not only that, but I was the only name on the mortgage, and no one else had that information, so it would have been impossible for anyone to make a payment on my behalf.

In addition, I had family and friends who took me to monthly, long-distance doctor appointments on weekends, during which they sacrificed their own family and rest time, as well as some paying for gas and food during the trip in order to help me. I also received small "refund" checks for accounts I had but didn't recall filing any applications requesting credits. During a day I spent trying to sell my jewelry to pay bills, I had missed lunch and obviously did not have the money to "eat out." At 3pm on my next-to-last stop at a pawn shop, I found $7 laying in the empty parking lot, at my feet when I got out of the car. I stopped by the few businesses nearby to see if anyone had lost the money, and no one had. God had provided the money for my lunch!

Long story short, God's faithfulness is without fail! By all logical deductions, I should have lost my home, gone without much-needed medical care, and ended up who-knows-where. But He made ends meet whenever needed and then some, and He comforted me during a time when I felt powerless to conquer my financial and physical challenges and loneliness. However, being in this wilderness also allowed me to apply what the Word had taught me about tithing; it taught me that there really is no excuse for refusing to offer whatever gifts you can to the Lord. If you are faithful, His grace is sufficient to meet your needs.

Please revisit the reasons and excuses you have for not tithing or donating financial gifts or other contributions to ministries by whatever means you have available. Consider that God doesn't ask for it because *He* needs it; it all already belongs to Him. He asks because our obedience draws us closer to Him through building of trust in His will and control over our own. Let go of your fear around your finances. Be generous with offering Him your intangible gifts as well. Bank on His plan and be confident that He can do infinitely more with your resources than you can.

Genesis 14:18-20 ❧ Malachi 3:8-10

Deuteronomy 14:22-23 ❧ Hebrews 10:26-27

Mark 12:41-44 ❧ Luke 6:38

Proverbs 11:24-25 ❧ Matthew 6:1-4, 21

WE DIDN'T WRITE THE BOOK

For those who follow Jesus, the Bible is accepted as the inspired, living Word of God and is full of wisdom and guidance intended to help us have a stronger, deeper and richer relationship with Him. The Lord leaves no room for mistaking or misunderstanding when He ends the Book of Revelation with a warning about adding to or taking away from His Word and the consequences for doing so.

Though Christians claim to read and believe the Bible, more and more of us have taken liberty with deciding what commandments, rules or instructions apply to us and which don't. We may not come out and say it, but how we live certainly reflects it.

Regardless of how we choose to dress it up, sin is sin, and we should not embrace and celebrate it at any level.

When we deny that our sin is evil, and actively and intentionally separate ourselves from the Lord, we are, in essence, telling Jesus that His horrific suffering and death were meaningless. When our human desires outweigh our interest in eternal life, we are consciously turning our backs on our Father's ultimate sacrifice. Christ is deemed unworthy of our attention, and salvation becomes an empty promise.

Our flesh is all about what's good for us. Society tells us to be the center of our own world and push back against anyone who challenges our microcosm of narcissism. The media encourages us to define our existence based on others' definitions, affirmations and approval instead of drawing our identities from the Holy Spirit within us and who we are in Christ. The internet, radio, TV and movies glorify ducking all personal accountability and living without appropriate and respectful boundaries and behavior on a grand scale. In short, we are beings made in God's image who have distanced ourselves from our Lord through our own choices. We are becoming the enemy's fodder by default, when it comes to picking and choosing which Biblical directives we consider acceptable.

God addresses many concerns in the Word. He tells us to be careful what we say regarding blasphemy, foul language, speaking negatively toward others, and lying. Keep in mind that lying includes exaggerating, embellishing, misrepresenting, and using half-truths. The Book of Proverbs is chock full of references to the misery caused by the tongue and its power to harm, or the benefits in its ability to lift up. We should be taking this instruction more seriously, instead of saying whatever we feel like saying because we believe we are entitled to do so.

God tells us that murder is wrong. Though He makes provision for accidental killings, He is very clear about taking a life out of hate, vengeance, or by way of lying in wait to do someone harm. Abortion is a sensitive subject for many, but the Lord does not condone murdering unborn children. Some Christians will argue about the right of a woman to choose the fate of these innocent souls, but regardless of how you frame it, murder is the intentional taking of a life. The circumstances surrounding these situations often involve people sinning by making decisions to engage in behaviors that casually create a miracle from God, and then destroy that life, probably because it was an inconvenience or was going to require a significant amount of effort, commitment, and money. There are always exceptions to these scenarios, but the majority of unwanted pregnancies stem from the pleasure derived from having sex outside of a covenant marriage.

Suicide is a sin. Some self-appointed authorities in Christian circles claim that taking one's own life is an unforgivable sin, but the Bible does not teach this. God says that His grace is sufficient, that Christ's sacrifice covers all sin for all time, but this doesn't give us permission to kill ourselves. Only God has the authority to determine when we are born and when we die. Free will provides man the option to murder himself, but it is not condoned by the Lord, and we will have to stand before Him and account for every aspect of our lives.

Sex in the Bible was a gift the Lord gave man to be shared between a husband and his wife for the purpose of showing physical affection, intimately bonding with each other, and conceiving children within marriage. God tells us that within the context of His design for marriage, the man and woman become unified (one flesh). It's not simply a physical pleasure; it represents a much deeper and sacred connection. Yes, of course it feels good because God wanted it to be a blessing to Adam and Eve and generations to come! However, the seriousness with which believers treat this holy covenant has been waning even since it began.

These days casual sex between people of all ages is becoming more common, andthe media has no problem displaying full nudity on TV shows and in movies. The Lord expressly addresses the human body as a temple for His Spirit…as something to be cherished, respected and covered out of modesty. However, God's teachings about sex have been diminished from generation to generation, and Christians are using their bodies to give themselves entertainment, comfort, and thrills instead of glorifying the Lord. With access to the internet, pornography has become poison in the mind of anyone who is interested in watching spiritually destructive filth. Some people have adopted these graphic videos and their manufactured worlds over trying to get out into the real world and have genuine relationships. They have been desensitized by the constant availability of carnal pleasure and its appeal of convenience, lack of effort required, being void of commitment, absence of self-control, immediate sexual gratification, and socially distancing oneself from meaningful connections with others. Sex-on-demand provides a plethora of sins in which people can indulge indefinitely.

Christians are also challenged by facing the issue of homosexuality. Again, the Lord is concise in the Bible about His opinion of this behavior. He specifically describes this practice differently than fornication or adultery. He calls it an "abomination" and perversion of His design and intent for sex. It is not how *we* feel or what *we* think that matters; only *God's* opinion matters! We are not to indulge in *any* sexual behavior outside of a covenant marriage.

As followers of Christ, we must learn to differentiate between qualities that are sacred and beyond our control (our ethnicity, skin color, family, who we are "on the inside" that only God will truly ever know, etc.) and the things we can control (our choice of thoughts, actions, words, beliefs, values, etc.). *Our state of being is not the same as what we decide to do, though today many people do not acknowledge the distinction.*

For instance, using foul language is a behavior common across cultures. Some people go right from the idea of the words to blurting them out without hesitation, whether out of habit or in the heat of an emotionally intense moment. They do not care about the impact that their intentional verbiage has (possibly to affect someone else) or flippant disregard for others' values and feelings when they are forced to listen to such nasty speech. In addition, those people probably fail to consider how that sinful behavior spiritually hurts them! In contrast, we have individuals who may think about using inappropriate language but take a moment to process the thought, weigh its value and consequences and choose not to sin by keeping themselves in check and remaining silent or choosing appropriate language. There is power in exercising these spiritual muscles and understanding that just because we have thoughts and feelings doesn't automatically mean that we should act on them. Our flesh will want to act; but we have the knowledge and authority to determine our path forward.

There is a reason that God emphasizes the importance of self-control in the Bible. We can be angry without becoming violent. We may desire to have "stuff" but should acquire it by paying for it versus stealing. Lust is ever-present but doesn't necessitate action. Our thoughts and emotions lay out the menu of options, but we, alone, are the ones who must discern which actions are pleasing to God and try to move in that direction.

Every person is a treasure to the Father and the apple of His eye—though each of us deserves His wrath when it comes to sin. Even the *greatest* non-Jesus role models are sinners. The type of sin, how many times we've sinned, or whether anyone knows about it or not is irrelevant to Jesus. He loves us just the way we are, including our personal baggage, imperfections and disregard for His gift of salvation. He is always available and eager to forgive and extend His mercy and grace to those who want to be part of His family.

In the Bible when Jesus healed the sick and worked miracles, He would often tell the recipient to "…sin no more." His recognition of the previous sin and instruction to change one's life to eliminate those behaviors are clear. He wants His presence in our lives to be more than a quick fix. He desires a new life for us, a clean slate, and a fresh start—a relationship that leads us to eternal blessings centered on His loving presence. We need only to believe, ask and repent! What an incredible gift!

If we are serious about the value of His gift, then *we do everything we can to avoid intentionally sinning.* If someone is a thief by nature, then he needs to try to sidestep tempting situations, whether frequenting stores, scanning for unlocked cars or picking through a supply closet at work where office items are available for the taking. If a parent is abusive toward her children or spouse, that person has the responsibility to seek professional help and keep a safe distance from her relatives until she has control over her behavior—even if that means finding a safe environment for the family until the threatening behaviors are under control. If a person is consumed by lust and is not in a covenant marriage relationship, that individual needs to find a Christian support group whose members can relate to fighting sexual impulses on a daily basis and who will give the encouragement and empathy necessary to help the person regain authority over their body and mind.

Regardless of the assistance that is available, two factors play key roles in creating a new reality from a sin-filled life. First, God must be at the center, because an individual's strength and discipline to change flows through Him. Second, a person must be repentant and want to change the sinful behavior. If people don't genuinely desire transformation in their lives, including lightening of their spiritual burdens and a fresh start, no number of strategies or interventions will work.

The Lord commands us to love others; *this does not mean that we are to praise, enable or endorse sinful behaviors.* The Apostle Paul put it succinctly when he wrote about not simply doing something that he could or wanted to do, because being able to do it didn't mean it was necessarily a positive thing. Christians have constant struggles to overcome, and we are responsible for not sabotaging our own spiritual family members by telling them it is okay to continue their "regular" sins and whatever they think is right. Consciously distinguishing our love for and support of all people from their choice to revel in sinful behavior is crucial to our walk with Jesus. I've heard it said to love the sinner but not the sin. However, man often has a hard time separating the two. We reject others instead of accepting who they are and encouraging them to step away from their sinful behavior. It doesn't have to be an all-or-none relationship.

We are supposed to use God's Word and discernment to hold each other accountable, working to strengthen our brothers and sisters in their faith—not by perpetuating the illusion that Christ is fine with self-indulgence and by delighting in our sins with only an occasional glance in His direction.

Mankind has tried to rewrite and manipulate the instructions in the Bible to suit its carnal self, but man cannot change the will of God. He has told us the truth and laid out the consequences, so we Christians cannot claim to be unaware of what awaits us when we finally stand before Him. We will also be liable for not attempting to help our family members who have lost their way.

Are you ready to look Him in the eye and account for your sins, particularly the ones you repeated habitually without concern or remorse? Will He smile and welcome you to His kingdom or turn His head away and say He never knew you?

God addresses many serious issues in the Bible and shares the wisdom we need for healthier lives. Our Lord wasn't obligated to write a book about who He is; He wrote it out of love. He tried to guide us in beneficial directions and warn us about the consequences of our sins, but how many Christians are listening? Or worse, how many of us have decided that God is wrong?

Numbers 23:19 ❧ John 2:13-16 ❧ Matthew 5:19-48

1 Peter 3:8-12 ❧ Ephesians 4:17-5:21 ❧ Luke 18:9-14

Micah 6:8 ❧ Zechariah 7:9-13

John 3:16-17 ❧ 2 Corinthians 5:10

SIMPLE DISCERNMENT

Do we really want to walk in God's will, or is the allure of the world's steady stream of mental, emotional, physical and spiritual fiction too persuasive?

The world says that we can do anything we set our minds to, all by ourselves, based on sheer will power and effort. Plenty of self-help resources affirm that we are the center of our world and can control it through self-sufficiency and planning.

The Lord debunks this philosophy repeatedly in the Bible as a form of self-worship and void of any true success. Utter reliance on Him precedes the ability to rise above failure through your personal skills and determination. His Presence strengthens and empowers us as He sees fit.

The world also feeds us a constant stream of glorifying sin and glamorizes its rewards. It does not acknowledge the negative consequences for our souls in the aftermath of sin's destructive wake.

Please consider the following responses to commonly accepted beliefs:

World's Belief

Consuming alcohol is attractive and relaxing, and drunkenness is fun, entertaining and socially desirable.

Bible Truths

"Who has woe? Who has sorrow? Who has contentions? Who has complaints? Who has wounds without cause? Who has redness of eyes? Those who linger long at the wine, those who go in search of mixed wine. Do not

look on the wine when it is red, when it sparkles in the cup, when it swirls around smoothly; at the last it bites like a serpent and stings like a viper. Your eyes will see strange things, and your heart will utter perverse things." Proverbs 23:29-33

"But they also have erred through wine and through intoxicating drink are out of the way; the priest and the prophet have erred through intoxicating drink, they are swallowed up by wine, they are out of the way through intoxicating drink; they err in vision, they stumble in judgment. For all tables are full of vomit and filth; no place is clean." Isaiah 28:7-8

"'But take heed to yourselves, lest your hearts be weighted down with carousing, drunkenness, and cares of this life, and that Day come on you unexpectedly. For it will come as a snare on all those who dwell on the face of the whole earth. Watch therefore, and pray always that you may be counted worthy to escape all these things that will come to pass and to stand before the Son of Man.'" Luke 21:34-36

World's Belief

As a Christian, incorporating occult practices and ideology into your life is okay.

Bible Truths

"'You shall not eat anything with the blood, nor shall you practice divination or soothsaying.'" Leviticus 19:26

"'Give no regard to mediums and familiar spirits; do not seek after them to be defiled by them: I am the Lord your God.'" Leviticus 19:31

"'And the person who turns to mediums and familiar spirits to prostitute himself with them, I will set My face against that person and cut him off from his people.'" Leviticus 20:6

"'When you come into the land which the Lord your God is giving you, you shall not learn to follow the abominations of those nations. There shall not be found among you anyone who makes his son or daughter pass through the fire, or one who practice witchcraft, or a soothsayer, or one who interprets omens, or a sorcerer, or one who conjures spells, or a medium, or a spiritist, or one who calls up the dead. For all who do these things are an abomination to the Lord, and because of these abominations the Lord your God drives them out from before you.'" Deuteronomy 18:9-12

"But he (Manasseh) did evil in the eyes of the Lord, following the detestable practices of the nations the Lord had driven out before the Israelites. He rebuilt the high places his father Hezekiah had demolished; he also erected altars to the Baals and made Asherah poles. He bowed down to all the starry hosts and worshiped them. He built altars in the temple of the Lord, of which the Lord had said, **'My Name will remain in Jerusalem forever.'** *In both courts of the temple of the Lord, he built altars to all the starry hosts. He sacrificed his children in the fire in the Valley of Ben Hinnom, practiced divination and witchcraft, sought omens, and consulted mediums and spiritists. He did much evil in the eyes of the Lord, arousing his anger.... But Manasseh led Judah and the people of Jerusalem astray, so that they did more evil than the nations the Lord had destroyed before the Israelites. The Lord spoke to Manasseh and his people, but they paid no attention. So the Lord brought against them the army commanders of the king of Assyria, who took Manasseh prisoner, put a hook in his nose, bound him with bronze shackles and took him to Babylon."* 2 Chronicles 33:2-6, 9-13

"So Saul died for his unfaithfulness which he had committed against the Lord, because he did not keep the word of the Lord, and also because he consulted a medium for guidance. But he did not inquire of the Lord; therefore, He killed him and turned the kingdom over to David the son of Jesse." 1 Chronicles 10:13-14

"Stand now with your enchantments and the multitude of your sorceries, in which you have labored from your youth—perhaps you will be able to profit, perhaps you will prevail. You are wearied in the multitude of your counsels; let now the astrologers, the stargazers, and the monthly prognosticators stand up and save you from what shall come upon you. Behold, they shall be as stubble, the fire shall burn them; they shall not deliver themselves from the power of the flame; it shall not be a coal to be warmed by, nor a fire to sit before!" Isaiah 47:12-15

"And Elijah came to all the people, and said, 'How long will you falter between two opinions? If the Lord is God, follow Him; but if Baal, follow him.' But the people answered him not a word. Then Elijah said to the people, 'I alone am left a prophet of the Lord; but Baal's prophets are four hundred and fifty men. Therefore let them give us two bulls; and let them choose one bull for themselves, cut it in pieces, and lay it on the wood, but put no fire under it; and I will prepare the other bull, and lay it on the wood, but put no fire under it. Then you call on the name of your gods, and I will call on the name of the Lord; and the God who answers by fire, He is God.' So all the people answered and said, 'It is well spoken.' Now Elijah said to the prophets of Baal, 'Choose one bull for yourselves and prepare it first, for you are many; and call on the name of your god but put no fire under it.' So they took the bull which was given them, and they prepared it, and called on the name of Baal from morning event till noon, saying, 'O Baal, hear us!' But there was no voice; no one answered. Then they leaped about the altar, which they had made. And so it was, at noon, that Elijah mocked them and said, 'Cry aloud, for he is a god; either he is meditating, or he is busy, or he is on a journey, or perhaps he is sleeping and must be awakened.' So they cried aloud, and cut themselves, as was their custom, with knives and lances, until the blood gushed out of them. And when midday was past, they prophesied until the time of the offering of the evening sacrifice. But there was no voice; no one answered, no one paid attention. Then Elijah said to all the people, 'Come near to me.' So all the people came near to him. And he repaired the altar of the Lord that was broken down. And Elijah took twelve stones, according to

the number of the tribes of the sons of Jacob, to whom the word of the Lord had come, saying, 'Israel shall be your name.' Then with the stones he built an altar in the name of the Lord; and he made a trench around the altar large enough to hold two seahs of seed. And he put the wood in order, cut the bull in pieces, and laid it on the wood, and said, 'Fill four waterpots with water, and pour it on the burnt sacrifice and on the wood.' Then he said, 'Do it a second time,' and they did it a second time; and he said, 'Do it a third time,' and they did it a third time. So the water ran all around the altar, and he also filled the trench with water. And it came to pass, at the time of the offering of the evening sacrifice, that Elijah the prophet came near and said, 'Lord God of Abraham, Isaac and Israel, let it be known this day that You are God in Israel and I am Your servant, and that I have done all these things at Your word. Hear me, O Lord, hear me, that this people may know that You are the Lord God, and that You have turned their hearts back to You again.' Then the fire of the Lord fell and consumed the burnt sacrifice, and the wood and the stones and the dust, and it licked up the water that was in the trench. Now when all the people saw it, they fell on their faces; and they said, 'The Lord, He is God! The Lord, He is God!' And Elijah said to them, 'Seize the prophets of Baal! Do not let one of them escape!' So they seized them; and Elijah brought them down to the Brook Kishon and executed them there." 1 Kings 18:21-40

World's Belief

There isn't anything special about your body or sex, so gratifying yourself in physical relationships outside of God's marriage covenant is acceptable and encouraged. Fornicate with anyone or anything you find appealing and convenient. It doesn't matter if they are single, married, in a relationship, related to you, have a variety of sexual preferences, or are animals.

<u>Bible Truths</u>

"Flee sexual immorality. Every sin that a man does outside the body, but he who commits sexual immorality sins against his own body. Or do you not know that your body is the temple of the Holy Spirit who is in you, whom you have from God, and you are not your own?" 1 Corinthians 6:18-19

"But fornication and all uncleanness or covetousness, let it not even be named among you, as is fitting for saints; neither filthiness, nor foolish talking, nor coarse jesting, which are not fitting, but rather giving of thanks. For this you know, that no fornicator, unclean person, nor covetous man who is an idolater, has any inheritance in the kingdom of Christ and God." Ephesians 5:3-5

"'You shall not lie with a male as with a woman. It is an abomination. Nor shall you mate with any animal, to defile yourself with it. Nor shall any woman stand before an animal to mate with it. It is a perversion.'" Leviticus 18:22-23

"…as Sodom and Gomorrah, and the cities around them in a similar manner to these, having given themselves over to sexual immorality and gone after strange flesh, are set forth as an example, suffering the vengeance of eternal fire." Jude 1:7

"For this is the will of God, your sanctification: that you should abstain from sexual immorality; that each of you should know how to possess his own vessel in sanctification and honor, not in passion of lust, like the Gentiles who do not know God." 1 Thessalonians 4:3-5

"Can a man take fire to his bosom and his clothes not be burned? Can one walk on hot coals and his feet not be seared? So is he who goes in to his neighbor's wife; whoever touches her shall not be innocent." Proverbs 6:27-29

<u>World's Belief</u>

Do anything that makes *you* feel good, regardless of its harmful impact on others.

<u>Bible Truths</u>

"But whoever has this world's goods and sees his brother in need, and shuts up his heart from him, how does the love of God abide in him? My little children, let us not love in word or in tongue but in deed and in truth." 1 John 3:17-18

"We then who are strong ought to bear with the scruples of the weak and not to please ourselves. Let each of us please his neighbor for his good, leading to edification." Romans 15:1-2

"Command those who are rich in this present age not to be haughty, nor to trust in uncertain riches, but in the living God who gives us richly all things to enjoy." 1 Timothy 6:17

*"Then He said to them all, **'If anyone desires to come after Me, let him deny himself and take up his cross daily and follow Me.'"*** Luke 9:23

"'Greater love has no one than this, than to lay down one's life for his friends.'" John 15:13

"Do not love the world or the things in the world. If anyone loves the world, the love of the Father is not in him. For all that is in the world, the lust of the flesh, the lust of the eyes, and the pride of life, is not of the Father but is of the world." 1 John 2:15-16

"In the measure that she glorified herself and lived luxuriously, in the same measure give her torment and sorrow; for she says in her heart, 'I sit as queen and am no widow, and will not see sorrow.' Therefore her plagues will come in one day—death and mourning and famine. And she will be utterly burned with fire, for strong is the Lord God who judges her." Revelation 18:7-8

<u>World's Belief</u>

Execute whatever justice you think is right. Taking matters into your own hands is justified.

<u>Bible Truths</u>

"Then David said to Abigail, 'Blessed is the Lord God of Israel who sent you this day to meet me! And blessed is your advice and blessed are you, because you have kept me this day from coming to bloodshed and avenging myself with my own hand.'" 1 Samuel 15:32-33

*"Beloved, do not avenge yourselves, but rather give place to wrath; for it is written, **'Vengeance is Mine, I will repay,'** says the Lord."* Romans 12:19

"O Lord God, to whom vengeance belongs—O God, to whom vengeance belongs, shine forth! Rise up, O Judge of the earth; render punishment to the proud. Lord, how long will the wicked, how long with the wicked triumph?" …. "He has brought on them their own iniquity and shall cut them off in their own wickedness; the Lord our God shall cut them off." Psalm 94:1-3, 23

"Evil men do not understand justice, but those who seek the Lord understand all." Proverbs 28:5

"It is not good to show partiality to the wicked or to overthrow the righteous in judgment." Proverbs 18:5

"Now therefore, let the fear of the Lord be upon you; take care and do it, for there is no iniquity with the Lord our God, no partiality, nor taking of bribes." 2 Chronicles 19:7

"'Woe to those who decree unrighteous decrees, who write misfortune which they have prescribed to rob the needy of justice, and to take what is right from the poor of My people. That widows may be their prey and that they may rob the fatherless. What will you do in the day of punishment, and in the desolation which will come from afar? To whom will you flee for help? And

where will you leave your glory? Without Me they shall bow down among the prisoners, and they shall fall among the slain.'" Isaiah 10:1-4

World's Belief

Lying, cheating, stealing, and clawing your way over others to pursue greed, power and fame is perfectly acceptable, and your family, friends, coworkers, acquaintances, and strangers who become collateral damage should be expected to fend for themselves.

Bible Truths

"These six things the Lord hates, yes, seven are an abomination to Him: a proud look, a lying tongue, hands that shed innocent blood, a heart that devises wicked plans, feet that are swift in running to evil, a false witness who speaks lies, and one who sows discord among the brethren." Proverbs 6:16-19

"'And you shall not glean your vineyard, nor shall you gather every grape of your vineyard; you shall leave them for the poor and the stranger: I am the Lord your God. You shall not steal, nor deal falsely, nor lie to one another. You shall not cheat your neighbor nor rob him. The wages of him who is hired shall not remain with you all night until morning. You shall not curse the deaf, nor put a stumbling block before the blind, but shall fear your God: I am the Lord. You shall do no injustice in judgment. You shall not be partial to the poor, nor honor the person of the mighty. In righteousness you shall judge your neighbor. You shall not go about as a talebearer among your people; nor shall you take a stand against the life of your neighbor: I am the Lord.'" Leviticus 19:10-16

"...Let the wicked be ashamed; Let them be silent in the grave. Let the lying lips be put to silence, which speak insolent things proudly and contemptuously against the righteous." Psalm 31:17b-18

"Whoever secretly slanders his neighbor, him I will destroy; the one who has a haughty look and a proud heart, him I will not endure." …. "He who works deceit shall not dwell within my house; He who tells lies shall not continue in my presence." Psalm 101:5, 7

"...Behold, the Lord comes with ten thousands of His saints, to execute judgment on all, to convict all who are ungodly among them of all their ungodly deeds which they have committed in an ungodly way, and of all the harsh things which ungodly sinners have spoken against Him. These are grumblers, complainers, walking according to their own lusts; and they mouth great swelling words, flattering people to gain advantage.'" Jude 1:14-16

<u>World's Belief</u>

Everyone goes to heaven when they die.

<u>Bible Truths</u>

"Nor is there salvation in any other, for there is no other name under heaven given among men by which we must be saved." Acts 4:12

*"Jesus answered and said to him, **'Most assuredly, I say to you, unless one is born again, he cannot see the kingdom of God.'"*** John 3:3

"He came to His own, and His own did not receive Him. But as many as received Him, to them He gave the right to become children of God, to those who believe in His name…." John 1:11-12

"Then one of the criminals who were hanged blasphemed Him, saying, 'If You are the Christ, save Yourself and us." But the other, answering, rebuked him, saying, "Do you not even fear God, seeing you are under the same condemnation? And we indeed justly, for we receive the due reward of our

deeds; but this Man has done nothing wrong.' Then he said to Jesus, "Lord, remember me when You come into Your kingdom.' And Jesus said to him, **'Assuredly, I say to you, today you will be with Me in Paradise.'"** Luke 23:39-43

"'Then He will also say to those on the left hand, 'Depart from Me, you cursed, into the everlasting fire prepared for the devil and his angels: for I was hungry and you gave Me no food; I was thirsty and you gave Me no drink; I was a stranger and you did not take Me in, naked and you did not clothe Me, sick and in prison and you did not visit Me.' Then they also will answer Him, saying, 'Lord, when did we see you hungry or thirsty or a stranger or naked or sick or in prison, and did not minister to You?' Then He will answer them, saying, 'Assuredly, I say to you, inasmuch as you did not do it to one of the least of these, you did not do it to Me.' And these will go away into everlasting punishment, but the righteous into eternal life.'" Matthew 25:41-46

"Then one said to Him, 'Lord, are there few who are saved?' And He said to them, **'Strive to enter through the narrow gate, for many, I say to you, will seek to enter and will not be able. When once the Master of the house has risen up and shut the door, and you begin to stand outside and knock at the door, saying, "Lord, Lord, open for us," and He will answer and say to you, "I do not know you, where you are from," then you will begin to say, "We ate and drank in Your presence, and You taught in our streets." But He will say, "I tell you I do not know you, where you are from. Depart from Me, all you workers of iniquity." There will be weeping and gnashing of teeth, when you see Abraham and Isaac and Jacob and all the prophets in the kingdom of God, and yourselves thrust out.'"** Luke 13:23-28

<u>World's Belief</u>

Christians are all hypocrites, so why try to be one?

<u>Bible Truth</u>

All people are hypocrites in different ways. No person is
perfect, nor will any of us ever be, including individuals who
follow Jesus. We struggle with sin, but the difference is that
believers strive not to sin and are truly sorry for our poor choices
and sinful behavior. Our desire to draw closer to the Lord helps
us in our fight against carnal nature, which creates the battle
between what we want to do and what we know we should do.
Our relationship with Christ strengthens us and opens our hearts
and minds to be used to share His love and light in the world. It is
not because of who we are, but because of who *He* is, that we can
be used as vessels of divine service. Being a Christian is standing
on a set of values and relationship that makes us want to share
God's Gospel hope with others, even if we deliver it in imperfect,
human, hypocritical packages.

<u>World's Belief</u>

The Bible is not written by God but by man and is not
accurate.

<u>Bible Truth</u>

The Bible was written by 40 people over approximately 1500
years and includes 66 books and over 31,000 verses about the
Lord's history, wisdom, knowledge and revelation. It clearly
teaches about who God is, His values, His laws, and the ultimate
sacrifice He permitted through His Son's death. Not only is the
Word accurate, but over time other texts have been discovered
that affirm its content. In theory, Christians believe the Bible's

teachings in their entirety. However, believers are still only human, and many, including religious and political leaders, have cherry-picked verses or twisted this holy text to read or infer whatever narrative best fits their self-serving purposes.

World's Belief

Christians think they are better than the rest of us.

Bible Truths

Christians are not better; we are set apart from nonbelievers because of our faith and should strive to behave in a manner that reflects God. The Word states that genuine followers of Jesus are free from the spiritual death that accompanies sin; we acknowledge that our sinful behavior is wrong and separates us from God. Our faith and repentance spare us from the consequences waiting for those who do not believe in Christ's being the Son of God, his suffering and death as payment for the world's sins, and our need for forgiveness.

Do you ever wonder why the world has such animosity towards Christianity? Perhaps, it is because Yahweh the Father, Jesus Christ, and the Holy Spirit are the only authority when addressing the definition of sin, explaining its origin, sharing why it is harmful and then offering salvation as a way to escape the spiritual consequences we truly deserve. No other belief system requires us to take ownership of our vast wrongdoing, repent and strive to become more like God. Only He provides the opportunity to receive eternal life in His presence through grace, which we cannot attain (no matter what we do) by ourselves.

For Christians, this path is exciting, and we cling to His promises with anticipation. But for the rest of the world, Christ's name casts light into their personal, hidden darkness filled with secrets, shame, pride, lust, greed, manipulation, sexual perversion, idol worship and other sins. They hate the holy illumination He exudes and will do anything they can to extinguish the revelation that it brings, including persecuting His followers. Evil cannot tolerate the hope, love and reminder of redemption that shines through Jesus' family.

As servants of God, we must decide with a strong "yes" or "no" to commit to His will. He says that the path to salvation is narrow, and that means that most people will make every excuse not to choose it. Will you?

TWISTING GOD'S DESIGN

Man has taken God's truth and design and contorted, corrupted, and perverted them into various philosophies and practices that go against His teachings and values. Some of these people are Christians, and believers have no business endorsing such ideas.

One aspect that has been twisted is understanding who Jesus is. We, as a church body, need to have compassion towards unbelievers (and believers who have drifted from their faith) and try to help them find answers for their questions and justifications as to why they do or do not have belief in or a relationship with the Lord. For instance, when people state that God can't possibly exist because of the pain and evil present in the world, we have been equipped to share with them that the Word explains how the world *was* once perfect and without these elements, but that sin invited pain and evil into it and affected all creation with the darkness it brought. Jesus offered Himself as a remedy for the harsh consequences that sin created. God's love working through us can help those who are lost discover the most amazing and unconditionally loving relationship in the world.

These conversations are essential for introducing faith and Biblical teachings to individuals who don't believe in God but blame Him for all the bad in the world; for providing clarity to those who claim Jesus was a person but say he was not the Son of God or resurrected; for shedding light on the importance of all people taking responsibility for their belief choices because not all people/faiths go to heaven; for correcting the rationalization that being a "good person" is enough to receive salvation; for explaining that worshipping—or revering as holy—people who aren't God (Buddha, Mohammed, Gandhi, Mother Teresa, the Pope, etc.) is a sin.

As brothers and sisters of Christ, we must be prepared to address situations that impact our spiritual family. This may include talking with church members who have adopted a faith paradigm that is a blend of philosophies or a lifestyle that is popular with their family and friends but not in alignment with Jesus' instruction. Some Christians are members of "religious" groups or similar organizations that use their faith to justify sinful actions (hate, violence, cruelty, death, greed, manipulation to create fear, etc.), none of which represent God's will. We also must guard against believers who promote systems that degrade and oppress specific populations, whether women, other minorities, the poor or any vulnerable citizens. It is the church's responsibility to acknowledge lovingly, but candidly, when its members are embracing sinful behaviors and address them.

The Human Race's worship of His gifts of science and the pursuit of knowledge is another aspect that constantly challenges God's design.. Although He bequeathed these tools to us for good, and some people use them appropriately, many others have not. Instead, they have pursued expanding their crania and aspire to elevate themselves to the level of ruler of the universe, or maybe just the world. Is it not enough that the Lord gave us charge over all His creation (including caring for one another)? Perhaps, man's desire to be more powerful or esteemed than his peers overrides his appreciation of what he has already been given.

Ironically, the most adamant denial of God the Creator comes from opponents' generation and endorsement of the "Big Bang Theory" script to explain how everything came into existence. However, scientific experts still cannot prove how something can suddenly and explosively come from nothing. Fictional narratives— that include many details and descriptions of particle activity—are available to justify this story, but none acknowledges the truth of creation—God spoke it into being.

Our fascination with science and knowledge has led to many amazing inventions and conveniences, but we have also used this information in ways that appear to sidestep the Lord's design. Genetic manipulation is one area that seems to involve playing God, whether it is trying to alter the genetic make-up of babies, changing genetic composition in our food to produce bigger and faster growing plants, selecting specific traits for animals and cloning experiments. We have also found ways around the inability of married couples to conceive children naturally. Today, individuals or couples do not need anything but access to fertility treatments, surrogate mothers, egg/sperm banks or other means by which to have a child outside of God's plan. Women can even order sperm in a syringe online and have it delivered to their homes to try and become pregnant! Many will claim that these discoveries and methods are all positive, but shouldn't we consider that maybe God does not "naturally" bless some people (both in covenant marriages and other relationships) with children via His design for one—or many—reasons)?

We have also twisted God's design in other areas. One such reality is using plastic surgery, extreme diet changes, medication, topical chemicals, over-exercising to the point of exhaustion, and whatever means necessary to fix everything we think is wrong or unattractive about ourselves. We equate physical beauty and the admiration of others as being more important than how God created us. (I am not including individuals who need surgery to help them gain or recover basic, necessary functions here.) Oftentimes, the identity we have as God's children—whom He adores—is skewed by the world's opinion and influences. There is no fault in wanting to live a healthy life *on your own terms*. Just remember that we are all *perfect* in His eyes!

Weapons are another product of science and knowledge that have advanced over the years to the point that the use of one bomb could forever impact the planet's stability and man's ability to survive on it. How did we get to this point when God instructed His followers to be peacemakers? It's because the majority of people on this planet are not interested in the Lord and His moral compass, but instead keeping what they have and acquiring more, including some Christians. The lust for power, land and control, coupled with the fear that someone else could seize another person's/country's autonomy, has driven humans to invent arsenals that are truly evil in concept and utilization. From military forces to private citizens around the world, man has access to all kinds of tools for suffering and destruction, from knives, guns, gas, mines, missiles, and biologic weapons to armored tanks, ships, planes and other delivery systems, to nuclear munitions, electronic disruptors, communication system hackings, wave/energy-based lasers and who knows what else.

To make things worse, many people believe that vengeance and justice (not the same) are theirs to deliver through violence. From a worldly perspective, we live in a no-win situation, which is why it is crucial that we reflect God's love and hope while we are here. He has already assured as that no weapon formed against us (believers) shall prosper against us (spiritually), so we needn't fear what the world fears. This world is not our home, but we will love and honor God, share His message and embrace people while we are here.

This chapter is far from exhaustive regarding God's design that man has reshaped to fit his own desires, but I think sex is definitely a subject that needs to be mentioned. (Since I've already described His plan in the chapter "We Didn't Write the Book," please reference that section for more details.)

So, based on simple observation, God created an intimate construct built on faith in Him, love and commitment to and from an equally yoked husband and wife, monogamy and the possibility of rearing children within this holy family. His design provided a dedicated spousal relationship that would (hopefully) provide a stable and nurturing environment for kids with the balance of knowledge, experiences, wisdom and affection from their father and mother.

When we step outside of that framework, everyone suffers from the sin that results, and sometimes it can create a domino effect of destruction. For instance, two people choosing to fornicate outside of a covenant marriage run the risk of getting sexually transmitted diseases. Should one or both of them contract an STD, it can be passed on (knowingly or unknowingly) to other sexual partners and can be fatal (AIDS). The woman also runs the risk of getting pregnant, and although there are couples who decide to get married and try to give their children a home, some women—or the men with whom they've had sex—decide that the baby will be aborted or abandoned. (Over 60 million abortions have occurred in the U.S. alone.) For women who decide to have the baby against the wishes of her sexual partner, they will become single parents who may or may not have support systems in place to help them rear their children.

Adultery between a single person and married person, or between two married—but not to each other—people is another domino sin. Not only is a person sinning against his/her own body in God's presence, but he/she is sinning against the person to whom they are married or the spouse of the person they are having sex with. God specifically speaks of making a husband and wife one flesh, so when one violates this promise, they are sinning in multiple ways. If a married person has children, then the affair impacts them as well.

Polygamy, bisexuality, homosexuality, bestiality or any other type of sex that is not covenant-marriage related is a sin. It doesn't matter how much you may love the person/people involved or believe that your circumstances are an exception to the rule. God's opinion is the only one that counts, and He clearly states in His word that His plan is holy. He doesn't lie, and He doesn't change His mind. Deciding that we disagree with His Word doesn't excuse the sin, regardless of our reasoning or attempted justification of it.

Since society has downplayed the sanctity of sex and the seriousness of sex-related offenses, many people (especially the young) have become victims of sexual crimes, including child abuse by "spouses" or other relatives, molestation by friends or acquaintances, kidnappings and rape as well as being sold into sex trafficking networks. Sex trafficking is currently an international crisis that has made abductions, sales and rape of children, teens and people of varying ages and sexes, commonplace. Child marriages are permitted in many countries, even though children should be protected by their parents until adulthood, when they are old enough to understand what marriage entails and make their own decisions. Pornography offers exploitation of people of all ages and provides sexual stimulation to whomever wants it via websites that encourage individuals to find sexual gratification without the need of another person.

For men, women and teens who are promiscuous, their casual encounters outside of marriage also contribute to their devaluation of modesty, decline of self-esteem/self-image, the loss of morals and desensitization to physical intimacy in relationships. Though Hollywood makes these lust-filled interludes seem romantic and appealing, casual sex is a temporary Band-aid for spiritual emptiness. Only God can fill the spiritual void that we seek; nothing in the physical world can.

These are only three areas which widen the huge spiritual chasm between the Lord and mankind every day. Though not complete lists by any means, the level of disregard that humans continue to show God and His guidance seems to grow effortlessly. We've decided that our carnal desires are more important than He is, and sadly, many people who think and feel this way are self-proclaimed Christians.

Believers are supposed to be vessels for God's light in this world. How can we shine His brightness and truth into the darkness if we accept and promote the darkness itself? We cannot have it both ways, and our doublemindedness will testify against us on the day we are judged. Will you honestly stand before the Creator who gave His Son's life; who sent numerous prophets to help, warn and empower us; who demonstrated many miracles, provided us with His Word and advocated for us with His Holy Spirit and try to justify why you accepted, supported, and/or participated in one or more of the behaviors or situations mentioned above? If so, be careful. Our faith is based on efforts to try to be more like Jesus, who offered forgiveness and told us to sin no more. How are you actively working towards sinning no more? *Are* you actively working towards sinning no more?

Genesis 1 ❧ Psalm 33:6-9 ❧ Romans 5:19-6:23

Deuteronomy 13:1-18 ❧ Luke 6:46 ❧ Exodus 32:1-35

2 Corinthians 6:14 ❧ Colossians 3:1-7

1 Corinthians 1:25-29 ❧ 1 Timothy 1:8-11

BOTH ENDS OF THE SPECTRUM

Father Jac Campbell was one of the most genuine, down-to-earth, humble priests I have ever met. I first became acquainted with him at my local church, when he subbed in for another priest who was out of town one weekend. My family discovered that his normal ministry was at a local university, where he held services for the students outside the rectory on the lawn. We opted to visit his service the following weekend and enjoyed the experience immensely. Some of the students brought guitars and a tall drum and created a make-shift area for a band. We were given a small sheet with lyrics on it, but the songs weren't traditional hymns, nor did the service have the rigidity that often accompanies Catholic ceremonies.

During the part of the service when we had come to expect a homily (sermon), Father Jac instead asked everyone (maybe twenty of us total) to find someone we didn't know and each spend ten minutes talking about where we needed prayers from them in our lives. He also offered to come and join us, if we needed the additional support or wanted him to pray with us. He drifted through the group, sometimes listening, often smiling and simply being present with people as they accessed a new-found, spiritual resource and friendship through their sharing. Gentle attentiveness and warmth flowed from him and invited you to relax, trust in your fellow brothers and sisters in Christ and be transparent about where you needed help. He was extremely effective in that he understood his role to be more about facilitating healing and faith through providing the opportunity for individuals to commune with God and each other through the mutual vulnerability that prayer requests presented. I was fascinated with how in touch he was with the Lord and people, not like many of his peers who were more focused on the routines and elevated status of their positions than the more intimate relationship I had sought (and not found) in the church growing up.

As I got older and was around him more, I realized that Father Jac completely owned his fallibility and didn't consider himself any more esteemed than the people in his congregation or community. Instead of telling people that they needed to confess their sins to him, he encouraged people to speak directly to God about the positive and negative aspects of their lives. He was a real person who had a sharp wit, told entertaining stories during his teachings, admittedly struggled with alcohol, was an active listener, gave healthy advice, possessed an average golf game, and who survived a heart attack to boot. Apparently, God had more projects in store for Father Jac!

Sadly, he was relocated by the church when I was 14. I missed him dearly, but our family kept in touch and visited with him whenever possible. He didn't let his new surroundings slow him down! He started an organization called *Landings International*, the purpose of which was to bring disenchanted Catholics back to the church for another look. Part of his philosophy was to acknowledge that the Catholic church did not have all the answers, and that no people within the church were perfect. He taught that we all need the Lord's mercy, and no person is above anyone else in the Lord's eyes. Christ looks upon each of us with the same love—no more, no less. Father Jac's reward for this pioneering effort was being ostracized and vehemently criticized by the church for promoting that church leadership was only human and that its longstanding methods weren't always effective. Nonetheless, he continued to cling to Jesus and tried to reach people, wherever they were in their lives, with unconditional acceptance and hope for the enriching of their faith. (Side note: The organization still exists today.) He admitted that he was a regular guy who was doing his best to help other regular people find the One who fills the unexplained emptiness in each of us. I can't wait to see him again in heaven, hug his neck and thank him for showing me God's wisdom and presence through his faith walk.

I would encounter the other end of the "Catholic" spectrum over a decade later, when I moved to Atlanta and got a job teaching at a parochial school. My new work family was a powerhouse of heart and intellect! The administrators, teachers and staff were phenomenal and passionate about their faith and the students' education, and we had found our groove! We earned the school's first accreditation with flying colors at the end of my first year, and I was excited with the anticipation of the next school year's adventures. Little did I know that they wouldn't be the promising growth of the institution or the celebration of our students' successes that I imagined.

After an agonizing political coup and a toxic change of administration, the school, as we knew it, was gone forever. The new administrators had crushed the soul of our efforts and our desire to empower our students through a rigorous academic program complemented by the healthy faith journey we offered— a path of support and encouragement alongside people who walked humbly before God. They had destroyed relationships, damaged many individuals' finances, inflicted physical and emotional harm to the students, families and staff—all wrapped in a package that claimed they were advocating for youth in the name of God—and made no apology for this travesty. They had their own manipulative schemes to execute, probably based purely on greed and power, after stealing *our* newly accredited organization (into which they, themselves, had put no effort), and those who wouldn't go along with their agenda became collateral damage.

Though my life experiences dealt with both ends of the spectrum regarding "Catholic" figures and institutions, the lessons apply to the "Christian" spectrum as well. Evil is everywhere, but we serve an awesome God who never leaves us. Please be aware that no matter what version of Christianity you may have been taught to believe, we are all only human. Your perspective will be colored by the types of people you encounter, especially people who claim to follow Jesus, so be careful. Seek those who do things in the light, base their walks on God's Word, do not mind being held accountable, display humility and humanness, admit their faults, apologize for wrongdoings, listen to wise counsel, are slow to speak, put others before themselves and whose faith produces fruit. Beware those who use the name of Jesus for personal gain and to edify themselves.

I got to love and appreciate a man through whom God moved to (I believe) bring significant increase to His kingdom, even though his fellow priests felt threatened by his light. Unfortunately, I also witnessed the chaos and destruction left in the path of men in positions of authority who thought they were almighty and who did things that exacerbated their many sins by claiming they were done "in the name God and the children." I'm not sure that those men and women were ever concerned about the eternal consequences for what they and their supporters did, but God sees everything, has a flawless memory and will show no partiality in His judgment. My prayer is that those individuals will humble themselves and repent before it is too late. Nonetheless, I trust His justice and am grateful for His faithfulness to His true family members. Regardless of the outcome here on Earth, we are and will continue to be favored, whereas the darkness will one day be destroyed...completely. Come, Lord Jesus!

Isaiah 5:18-24 ❖ Ephesians 2:2-3, 5:11-12 ❖ John 3:19-21

John 10:10 ❖ 2 Corinthians 6:14–7:1 ❖ Proverbs 8:13

1 John 2:1-6 ❖ Psalm 37:7-17

CHOOSE YOUR WORDS CAREFULLY

Society has really watered down its scale of what is defined as offensive language over the years. Decades ago, you wouldn't hear the profanity that has become commonplace in Hollywood and accepted as normal in the real world. But verbal filth is flaunted and perpetuated in our media, whether on billboards, bumper stickers, TV, the Internet, the radio, or the big screen.

As followers of Jesus, we must be diligent to guard our tongues and measure the use of our words against His teachings and warnings of their sinful consequences. Obviously, today's variety of curse words range from foul to graphic to just plain mean. None of these terms or phrases foster positive influence and mutual respect for our fellow man. The worst language one can use is the taking of the Lord's name in vain. Yes, it's difficult to find a TV show or movie that doesn't casually, but forcefully, drop a "Jesus C*****" or "God d***" on a regular basis. As difficult as those curses are for Christians to hear, there are many believers who routinely utter these anti-God sentiments themselves, whether through anger or habit.

The Father's command that "Thou shall not take the name of the Lord in vain" was not a suggestion. He is almighty and holy, yet His name is now used as an afterthought when something goes wrong. Imagine, for a second, if someone cursed using OUR name every time they had a crisis, inconvenience, surprise, or another type of event that triggered their frustration, fear, anger, hatred or sadness. How would we feel to have our name constantly inserted into human suffering and misery when it had nothing to do with us? Now, put yourself in God's shoes: the shoes of the only true, loving, compassionate, merciful Jehovah, who is perfectly righteous and sacrificed His Son to pay for our sins. When we curse using His name, we are basically disowning our royal inheritance. This perspective is one of the most spiritually destructive positions a person can assume—to deny the ultimate Gift by flippant and malicious use of His name.

Then, let's not forget ideas or phrases that endorse power and authority other than the Lord's. For instance, many people say, "Good luck!" all the time. Wake up, folks! Luck is NOT real! There isn't some mysterious entity in the universe with its own way of determining whether you will succeed or fail in your endeavors. Leprechauns are make-believe. Black cats have no power. Wood surfaces are not imbued with the ability to keep bad things from happening. Ladders are simple equipment that can be potential hazards when left in busy areas. Mirrors break due to physics and carelessness. Sidewalks will have cracks on them, but these features do not affect the health of your loved ones.

Astrology is make-believe, yet some people feel compelled to read their horoscope each day in great expectation of it prophesying their destiny. The planets' alignment or movement is not a valid explanation or justification for people's behavior. If you find money on the ground, it doesn't matter what side of a coin is turned up…it is only money and has no power! Numbers, like 13, don't have a secret will of their own, so *be careful* that you keep those words or thoughts out of your vocabulary.

The Lord has given us power in what we say, but He intended for our tongues to express the truth about Him, His love for us, encouragement for others, and to be used in prayer. He is not interested in our minds embracing and promoting lies about the origin of power or giving credit to people, objects, animals or locations as having natural authority when they don't.

We should remove the word "karma" from our vocabulary. This concept is pure idolatry. The universe is a created space with an amazing and unique ensemble of heavenly bodies, various life forms, many different habitats, unexplored realms, and a multitude of things from microscopic to huge-beyond-measure, that we cannot begin to explain. This phenomenal expanse of majestic design in which we live does not have a personality or a plan, and it certainly doesn't have any self-awareness or capability of keeping tally marks on an imaginary scoreboard for every positive or negative things we've done in our lives.

Man thought up that concept which is rooted in a religion that does not believe in our Trinity. "What goes around, comes around" is not a Biblical principle. We believe in an existence based on our relationship with God and trusting His oversight of our lives to be for our highest good. He never promised an equal balance of celebrations and challenges. He simply tells us that we (believers) will reap what we sow, and He will be with us all our days. The result of our decisions and His will shall unfold at His discretion. The comfort is in knowing that He is always faithful to His family. This concept does not apply to the rest of the world who are not interested in the Lord; it only provides for those of us in a relationship with Him.

Complaining is another practice we need to avoid. When we grumble about our circumstances, we push aside our appreciation for God's blessings and focus on what we think is lacking in our lives or situations. Sometimes, we begin to entertain in our minds how *we* would have done things differently or better if we were in the Lord's position. We may not be happy with whatever is going on, but we need to be careful about vocalizing our discontent and disrespecting God with our absence of gratitude or critical thoughts regarding how He chooses to act (or not).

Finally, remember the Lord's words regarding evil flowing out of a man's heart through his words. We have enough evil running rampant in the world without Christians adding to it. Wisdom means checking our hearts and minds before we speak to see if our intentions and words line up with scripture. We are to reflect God's radiance and use it to brighten our world.

So, choose words carefully, because He will hold us responsible for each and every one when our days here are finished. What will our words say about us?

Matthew 12:34-37 ✜ Luke 12:2-5

James 3:3-6, 9-12 ✜ Proverbs 13:2-3

Philipians 2:14-15 ✜ Colossians 3:8-10 ✜ Isaiah 29:13

ARE YOU STANDING?

Now, more than any other time in history, the enemy is whittling away at the world's desire to be in communion with God. The Bible repeatedly refers to his motives as being to steal, kill, and destroy in a futile effort to take God's place. Yet many Christians open the door (both actively and passively) to welcome in the devil's anti-Christian behaviors without giving them much thought. Are you standing on God's promises and against the prevalence of evil?

For instance, I know extremely faith-filled people who, when upset, often use "God d***!" or "Jesus C*****!" as expletives. It makes me wonder how people who deeply invest in their relationship with the Lord would habitually curse using His name and see nothing wrong with it. Are we speaking up and letting these individuals know that this disrespectful language is offensive to those of us who are followers of Jesus? Or are we remaining silent and passively reinforcing such expressions as permissible?

Not only do we let verbal utterances slide, but many Christians allow other inappropriate behaviors to go unchecked as well. True believers will call out this hypocrisy and distance themselves from people consistently exhibiting words and actions that go against the Lord's instruction. We are told to pray for these individuals but not to associate with or encourage their destructive and sinful behaviors. No one is sin-free, but genuine followers of Jesus will be held accountable for their sins as well as their complicity in enabling others to indulge in sin. We are expected to correct our spiritual kin using Biblical principles and teachings, so we cannot turn a blind eye to situations and people that make us uncomfortable. The Lord has told us to stand up against evil, no matter its form. He is counting on believers to intercede on behalf of our brother and sisters in Christ and our neighbors against the seduction and gratification of this world. Some anti-Christian efforts are subtle and sneaky, and Christians are not immune from these spiritual infections and influences.

Blatant attacks on churches and our freedom to worship the Lord also seem to result in quite a few Christians remaining silent, whether out of fear or apathy. Do not stay quiet! Speak out and with God's authority to defend our passion and right to celebrate the One true Lord! Our Creator did not command us to go forth and cower at the world's criticism and condemnation, but to share His Good News—the Gospel of Christ—and His desire that all should be saved. We need to use our voices to bring light at a time when darkness threatens to consume mankind. The Lord is ready and eager to battle on our behalf, as long as our confidence is in Him.

God arms us with His Spirit and calls us to stand on His promises, relying on what He has already said will be. He empowers us to counter the world's deception, comfort the suffering, speak the truth, use His words, share His love, accept His grace, trust His will, and spread Jesus' eternal legacy of hope.

Are you courageous enough to be more than a silent witness to this crucial time in our world's history? God *placed us here* right now, and we are the ones who must stand for God's teachings and share His truth when others won't.

Are we Christians whose foundation and beliefs are based steadfastly in the Lord's truth, or does our faith easily falter when conflicts arise?

2 Chronicles 20:1-30 ❧ Acts 5:12-42 ❧ Galatians 5:19-26

2 Corinthians 12:5-10 ❧ Ephesians 6:10-20

2 Timothy 2:11-13 ❧ 1 Corinthians 10:13 ❧ Romans 8:37-39

What's on the Menu?

In the Old Testament God spoke at length about what food and drink the Israelites should abstain from consuming and/or how much was permitted or recommended. He was very specific as to which animals were permissible and those that should be excluded from one's diet, all based on what He knew to be healthiest for them. The only blanket restrictions put on food were on that which was prepared and eaten outside their homes/community (like at another person's dwelling, which contained blood or had been sacrificed or offered to idols) and specific dishes eaten during holy days. He also repeatedly commanded His followers not to be gluttons but to eat in moderation.

Although many Jews continue to honor the Lord's commands regarding their diet, Christians are not bound by the Old Covenant. Jesus died for our sins and was the final sacrifice for the world's salvation. He reiterated His Father's instructions about avoiding blood and food involved in idol worship, but He did not put any limitations on plant or animal consumption. As a matter of fact, Christ emphasized that it is not what a man puts into his body, but what comes out of his heart, that defiles him. Spiritual matters trump the physical ones when it comes to our walk with the Lord. You can adopt the healthiest nutritional regiment on the planet, but if your heart is toxic and miserable, your words and actions will follow suit. He does not forbid us to eat any fruit, vegetable, nut, seed, meat, fish, or other food in general or based on "Christian holidays." "Christian" rules about diet are manmade, not God-made.

Another point Jesus made regarded an individual's faith. If a person honestly believes that eating or drinking a specific food or beverage hinders his faith or walk with God, do not encourage that person to change his mind or habit regarding that practice. If they see it as a stumbling block to their journey, then it is. Though this perception may not be true in terms of the Lord's teachings about being permitted to eat from what He has supplied, God honors their efforts to draw closer to Him. He does not want other believers interfering in that precious relationship, when those ideas are harmless to self and others, and are practiced out of honor and respect for Him. The Lord considers the heart first and knows the motivation for all our actions.

In the book of Acts, Peter experiences a vision during the day that also addresses the idea of consuming animals. In it, God tells him that no animal is considered unclean and that he can kill and eat any of them, because the Lord has cleansed them all.

*"The next day, as they went on their journey and drew near the city, Peter went up on the housetop to pray, about the sixth hour. Then he became very hungry and wanted to eat; but while they made ready, he fell into a trance and saw heaven opened and an object like a great sheet bound at the four corners, descending to him and let down to the earth. In it were all kinds of four-footed animals of the earth, wild beast, creeping things and birds of the air. And a voice came to him, **'Rise, Peter; kill and eat.'** But Peter said, 'Not so, Lord! For I have never eaten anything common or unclean.' And a voice spoke to him again the second time, **'What God has cleansed you must not call common.'** This was done three times. And the object was taken up into heaven again."* Acts 10:9-16

So, except for the aforementioned forbidden foods, "Bon Appetit" as you see fit!

Leviticus 11:1-47 ✣ Daniel 1:3-16 ✣ Proverbs 23:20-21, 25:16

Matthew 15:17-20 ✣ 1 Corinthians 8:1-13, 9:27, 10:25-31

REALITY AIN'T WHAT IT USED TO BE

My freshman year of college, I unknowingly signed up for the coolest, hardest class I would take during my four-year education. *Intro to Logic* was an ominous course for those who knew better than to sign up, since it could easily put a dent in your GPA. Dr. Gerald Shinn ended up being my favorite professor! He wasn't interested in the status quo, being popular or worrying about whose toes might get stepped on. He made it his mission to challenge how you thought, not just what you thought or why. I have always remembered something he said in our first class, "Believe none of what you hear, half of what you read, and only what you see if you are present to witness it firsthand." At the time (pre-internet), I couldn't believe he had such a negative perspective of how people acquired accurate information. However, over the last 30 years, his advice has rung true—even more so with the technological advances that have become available.

Fast forward a decade, when I discovered that someone I knew had been contracted to participate in a TV program which was a "reality" show. She wasn't allowed to talk about it at the time (due to her legal agreement—the logic of which I didn't really understand until later), but when years later she *could* tell me about it, I was shocked! When she was finally able to disclose the details, she described a nightmare that was far from the real world. The opposite of "reality," it was actually scripted and rehearsed and performed over and over again, with the parts then spliced together to create the "story" the producers wanted the audience to believe. Producers also dubbed dialogue over various scenes to misrepresent the actual content.

First, she explained how every scene of the show/season was filmed in tiny, impersonal bits. If there was a scene in the kitchen, for instance, she was told to enter and say her line in a happy mood; then to do it again in a sad mood; then do it again in an angry mood; then do it again in a confused way; then with hysteria; then dismissive; then frustrated; then helpless; then violent. You get the picture. These scenes were then cut together with her costars' similar segments to create the narrative with as much conflict as possible, in whatever way the show producers thought would draw the most viewers covering various demographics.

Unlike movies and TV shows that everyone *knows* are fictional (and don't claim to be otherwise), these shows claimed to reflect real-time, everyday life but were actually well-choreographed lies. It was a nightmare for these star-gazing Hollywood hopefuls who had signed up not realizing—until it was too late—that they had legally obligated themselves to become puppets being used to create a false story, and they had no freedom to say or do anything to help themselves or tell the public what was going on.

Due to her contract, my friend was not permitted to discuss the way the show was constructed until the mandated period of confidentiality ended, or she and her family could be taken to court and financially ruined forever. She and other participants were threatened because the lie could not be revealed to the public, or it would ruin the big money and popularity that reality shows generated. This may explain why so many current and former reality show stars' struggles become newsworthy—because of their ignorance of the process and consequent misery and inability to deal with the destructive environment and the deceptive product of their efforts.

After the show ended and aired, she received other "reality" show offers but declined them, since she was now aware of how they worked.

Today, reality shows are a dime a dozen, but the saddest part is that the audience *actually believes they are real.* I have spoken to people who became angry at me when I shared my friend's experience with them. How when she went through this—what appeared to be an exciting—opportunity, it was extremely traumatic and misrepresented the individuals' genuine experiences. When she told others about this part of her life, many criticized her and unfriended her on Facebook, not wanting to hear the truth of the illusion their minds had come to embrace and enjoy. They wanted to protect and defend these manufactured storylines rather than thanking her for revealing the deception to them or praising her courage, truth-telling and desire to maintain their healthy friendships with her. When she did interviews with media outlets to alert viewers to what was going on behind the scenes, somehow her negative comments and warnings were edited out, and only the most mundane and harmless elements of the conversation were used. (Are you getting the REAL picture yet????)

My peers have even tried to justify to me why they watch or record certain reality shows that are based on their own values and interests. Hollywood's window dressings have something to draw everyone in, regardless of the topic. There are even channels that play nothing but reality shows. Sadly, I don't know which is worse—the media's effort to conceal the lie and perpetuate it as truth, or the public's denial of—and distaste for—it if/when they do find out.

Let's just say I have come to appreciate Dr. Shinn's wisdom over the last three decades of seeing how easy it has become to manipulate things that are seen, heard or printed. Little did my favorite professor know that things could get so much worse—or how quickly!

During my college years, the tech curve was transitioning into the development and applications of the internet. We were fascinated and excited by how useful and convenient this new creation was! However, we now had a tool that could effortlessly feed people information in a few seconds without having to demonstrate any proof as to its validity. (Back in the old days, we used to accomplish this via a process called "doing research" which involved libraries, card catalogs and "the stacks" of reference materials.) These days, viewers can get TV shows, movies, personal videos and other selections projected into their homes and onto a variety of devices at the press of a button. Unlike years ago, many people do not question the truth of what they see on the internet or the source, since they simply *believe* it must be correct. This platform enables anyone to say, write, read or do whatever they desire without accountability.

Unfortunately, in the beginning not enough people were concerned with policing the system for harmful material or false communications, so it has become an uncontrolled source of inappropriate social interactions, where people feel free to express whatever they want because they are protected by anonymity or the claim of free speech. A significant number of sites seem to be a constant stream of misinformation that gets people riled up, distracted, and emotionally off-balance—both on the internet and the dark/deep web.

Our tech has also increased personal exposure and vulnerability regarding any financial transactions and personal data that we upload or keep filed on personal computers or in institutional databases. In addition, this medium offers predators channels through which they can physically harm others via sex trafficking or targeting victims based on their posted activities, like luring young people into dangerous and compromising situations, kidnappings, breaking into people's homes when they are on vacation, attacking individuals who meet to sell/buy goods and other twisted and evil uses.

Long story short, we as Christians need to consider where we are getting our information! What is the source of our truth? Are we relying on a fallible, manmade system which is useful but also *very* manipulative, to deliver our facts to us, or do we understand that Dr. Shinn's advice is more valuable today than it was years ago? Have we let search engines replace God's Word? Are we giving credibility to technology over faith? Have we allowed this tool to distract us to the point that we are spending less time seeking things of real value and letting it destroy our perspective and relationships? Are we really interested in getting control of our minds and feelings and directing our focus to the Lord as well as helping our fellow man, versus allowing the tide of misinformation to toss us to and fro on the ocean of poisonous political agendas? Do we have the strength to acknowledge that for the most part society now worships the convenience and entertainment of our tech to the point that people will become almost rabid if that source is threatened? Do we have the courage to reject the spiritual garbage that the devil loves providing to us through simple clicks and swipes?

People of God, please wake up! Please ground yourself in facts that do not change: in a God who never changes. Please turn off the lies and deception and connect with your brothers and sisters in Christ. Find reconciliation and restoration of your minds in Him. Though tech has the power to share the Gospel in ways we never could until now, be aware that it can also perpetuate the illusion of wisdom and power, religious myths, faulty "knowledge," and false sources of hope. But we have Jesus—the only *real* Hope.

Psalm 52:1-5 ✂ 1 Timothy 4:1-2 ✂ 2 Thessalonians 2:9-12

Ecclesiastes 12:14 ✂ Colossians 2:8

PRAYER IS...

As I write this, I am closing in on a significant milestone birthday, and one thing I've discovered in these decades is what prayer is and what it isn't. These observations do not demonstrate that I have some sort of divine introspection; these thoughts come from my reading of God's Word and life experience.

According to the Lord, He values time alone with us. The Bible indicates that we should seek quiet places where we can be still and focused as we commune with Him. This speaks of intimacy...that our Father desires to share our most secret thoughts, struggles, dreams and successes through our relationship. Though He already knows it all, He wants us to draw closer to His presence and enjoy His undivided attention and affection. We are His family, His most precious creation, the perfect bride for His holy Son.

God also finds pleasure in our spending time in prayer with other believers. His Word tells us that He is always present when two or more Christians are gathered in His name. This time of fellowship is not intended to be a display of faith for the benefit of nonbelievers but a time of praise to God and mutual spiritual support for our brothers and sisters in Christ. Intercessory prayer (on behalf of others) is a powerful weapon against the enemy, as is anytime we pray for the Lord's will above our own.

The Bible also repeatedly mentions how God treasures thanksgiving in combination with our prayers. Simply put, we need to remember and honor what blessings and mercies He has already given us before we dive into our current list of requests or concerns. When I taught middle school, I had a poster in my room that I left up year-round to remind me of that same principle. It read, "Give more than you take." I think it reflects a healthy spiritual perspective of the type of rapport we should aim to have with our Father. Many people only turn to Him when in a crisis or to make self-centered demands versus offering gratitude or praying for the well-being of others.

I'm not saying to ignore or forego our own prayer needs and requests, but they shouldn't dwarf our awareness of the awe-inspiring presence of God or the needs of others, especially those who are members of our spiritual family. Man's natural tendency leans toward "Me, first," so we have to make a concerted effort to remember that Jesus told us to love God above all else, and love our neighbors as we love ourselves. This means we champion others' needs as aggressively as we do our own, both in prayer and in our everyday lives. Intercessory prayer lifts up our brothers and sisters in the spiritual realm, bringing our intentions into line with God's will for their lives and blessing them through our faith. We need to be diligent in sowing the power that the Holy Spirit gives us into our kingdom family's struggles and suffering. This focus should not only be on our family and friends but also include missionaries around the world and members of the persecuted church whose lives and families are in constant danger of physical harm and death due to their belief in Jesus. Are we asking the Lord to protect them, provide whatever they need, encourage and strengthen their spirits and sustain their passion for loving His Son and spreading the Gospel message?

Prayer is sometimes messy. God expresses His desire for us to communicate genuinely with Him from our hearts which means that our thoughts and words might come out in un-choreographed and spontaneous, emotional ways. He doesn't want to hear chanting, or memorized, repeated prayers like those spoken by people who worship idols, including the devil. Think about it. How would you feel if you came home to a relative or friend every day and that person repeated, word-for-word, mechanically and without any particular amount of eye contact or affection, the conversation you'd shared every single day since you first met? No *real* thoughts, feelings, worries, praises, hopes, dreams, pain, emotions, or challenges other than whatever was in that single dialogue. *That* is a broken record! Yet, many people talk to God on autopilot all the time! Jesus never instructed anyone to behave this way. I imagine that it is heartbreaking for God to have children who have no interest in sharing the nitty gritty reality of being human and not wanting to connect with Him other than using these token, lifeless scripts.

Prayer is not a demonstration to show the world how "religious" or faith-filled you are. Jesus warns us about the religious leaders of His day (and ours) who pray with many words in the presence of others to try to prove their piety and closeness to God. He calls them out for using empty words and displaying behavior that is hypocritical of individuals who were supposed to be modeling for—and spiritually guiding—the common man. Your private prayers with your Father should only be known to others through the light He chooses to shine on them via your willing heart.

Prayer is an opportunity to be totally transparent with every part of who you are with your loving Father. He is not hovering there looking down His nose at you, waiting for you to stumble through what you have to say. He is patiently attentive and ready for you to sit on His lap while He listens to you share your soul. This may mean moments of laughter or tears, depending on your life's journey. Anger, grief, frustration, joy, excitement, anticipation and more may flow from your lips as you spend time with Him. The special communion is a blessing to you both. You may find that prayer allows you to shut out the world while reaching out to listen for His whispers to you. You might find that

His peace envelops you as you deepen your trust, with your feelings of fear or vulnerability fading away. He loves you, no matter what!

Prayer is not a punishment. So, if someone tells you that in order to receive forgiveness you must pray "x, y, and z," it is a lie. Jesus said that He is the only Way, Truth and Life: the only path to the Father. As the Son of God and only authority in the church, He *never* gave His disciples a checklist for grace, nor did He demand repetitive regurgitation of "prayers." This methodology was created by man to insert his own hierarchy of power and control over faith into God's perfect plan, something that the Lord does not want, need, or condone. We can go straight to our King and talk to Him whenever we want and without anyone else's permission or involvement. Jesus's death opened that door for us, and no one can try to manage or close it! Our Father is available 24/7—without condition—to spend time with us!

Prayer is holy and is only between God and you. Everyone and everything else are *not* God and are therefore created beings or objects. We are not supposed to pray to creation of any kind: not to Jesus' earthly family (Mary, Joseph, etc.), nor to His Apostles, the angels, saints, our deceased relatives, "religious" rulers, plants, animals, oceans, the moon or sun, planets, nature, the sky, or anyone/anything else. None of these people and things have power or authority of themselves, and they do not determine the course of the universe or our lives. God is the only One who receives and responds to our prayers, and these intimate conversations are of infinite value to Him. Imagine having a best Friend who treats your every thought as a protected secret! He IS that Friend!

Prayer cannot ever make things worse, so have no fear about what you say being "wrong." Speak from your heart and be assured that the Holy Spirit will help you find the words, when needed. Your Father does not dictate how you must pray; He enjoys time that you spend with Him, whether speaking, listening or simply being still. A child might have a tantrum and say hateful things, but the Father is always faithful. A child can be lost in pain and drowning in sorrow, but our Father never leaves us. His compassion and comfort are always nearby. A child may turn his back and deny being part of God's family, but God remains loving and watchful even when the child chooses to leave. It is man's choice not to believe that separates him from God's grace, so nonbelievers actively choose not to have access to the favor and forgiveness which flows through Jesus.

The Lord was, is and will always be available for those who seek Him without rules or restrictions. Let your prayers flow and draw you closer to Him. He is ready to listen.

Matthew 6:5-8 ❧ Jeremiah 29:12-13 ❧ Luke 18:1-8

James 5:13-18 ❧ Philippians 4:6-7 ❧ Luke 22:39-46

SPIRITUAL SUPERPOWER

Being a Christian is a supernatural experience, not because we are made any different than other people, but because of how the Lord chooses to move through us with His power, wisdom, love, and grace. His presence provides abilities that go completely against our fleshly tendencies and emotions.

Forgiveness is a holy gift, and humanity struggles with the concept. In a world and U.S. culture overrun with fierce tension, animosity, and blatant racism and discrimination, we are in desperate need of the discipline of forgiving one another. We also experience many types of accidents and circumstances, the results of which may cause injury or death. Our knee-jerk reactions to wrongs committed against us often manifest as angry words and violent reactions, defense mechanisms to the attacks to our person, reputation, families, careers, or beliefs. Forgiveness is typically the last option that many consider after being the victim of provocation and assault, whether verbal, physical, or some other kind. It is counterintuitive and certainly flies in the face of our human instincts for self-preservation and retaliation. That is why it is a superpower.

Only the Lord could provide people the opportunity for such profound, spiritual metamorphosis! He has already told us that He will transform every action intended for evil against us into something that will benefit us. When we forgive those who sin against us, not only are we trusting God with our pain and suffering, we affirm our belief in His perfect and righteous judgment. The Bible does not tell us to forget these events, but it does instruct us to forgive *everyone*—over and over and over again. In Christ's words, "seventy times seven times." Our Savior can request this of His church because He already paid the price for mankind's sins for all time. Take a moment to consider that cost: an estimated 117 billion people have existed. Multiply that number by a very conservative estimated average of 7,000 sins in a person's lifetime equates to over *858 trillion sins' worth of punishment due and growing every minute.* (Note: I lowered the estimated average because of the number of people who die before adulthood or at a young age due to their life circumstances.) Yes, finding the willingness to forgive and genuinely mean it takes strength and determination beyond our natural state of being.

But the Lord doesn't ask anything of His family that is beyond our reach *with His assistance.* Jesus has placed forgiveness within us, if only we choose to use it. If we don't show the world the power of God's love in times of crisis—even when hostility or hatred may be directed at us—how will nonbelievers ever come to understand the mystery of our Father's forgiveness of those who murdered His only Son, or Jesus' mercy on those who killed Him? Are you showing others the power of forgiveness that flows from your faith, or are you holding fast to grudges and unforgiveness in your heart?

Matthew 18:21-22 ❧ Micah 7:18-19 ❧ Psalm 32:1, 103:11-14

Ephesians 1:7-8 ❧ Isaiah 55:7 ❧ Proverbs 28:13

UNWAVERING LOYALTY

Loyalty is a rare quality, especially with relationships. Fewer and further between are the number of employees who have long-term dedication to a company and vice-versa. Deep friendships are hard to develop, and loyalty has become an "old-fashioned" concept that isn't honored much anymore.

However, the Lord is loyalty perfected! No matter how knock-down/drag-out the world becomes, He maintains His faithfulness to us. Regardless of who tosses us to the side or what tragedy indiscriminately strikes, He is there. God is always here because that's who He is and promises to be for His children forever. He is the Unconditional Love we crave and the only One who can fill the hollowness in our being.

Even now, Jesus is preparing places for believers in His Father's house in heaven. How cool is that? The Bible tells us that the God who created time and space and knows all things wants us to be aware of His plans to live with us forever. He doesn't share these housekeeping items with us out of obligation but out of His affection for our souls. The Holy Spirit was given to God's children so that we wouldn't ever be without the Lord's presence. He guides, protects, provides for and comforts believers, enabling us to enjoy our relationship with the Lord 24/7 without interruption. He is not fickle and only available at His whim; He is dedicated to every moment of our lives.

In heaven we will rejoice in the majesty of being able to look upon His face, experiencing the gift of new bodies, and existing without any stressors, worry, or pain. But life on Earth is quite different. Although we have celebrations and successes to cheer, the Bible quotes Jesus as saying that we *will* have trials of all sizes to weather and overcome. Our peace does not lie on the other side of these traumatic events but in our Savior and Companion who holds us in His right hand and hugs us close as we move through them.

God is not as preoccupied with our past as we are. He is more interested in where you are right now and the state of your faith and struggles moving forward. He is here, praying for us, waiting with us, showering us with fiercely loyal love.

So, if you are depressed, diseased, lost, longing, isolated, ostracized, persecuted, suffocating, poor, oppressed, abandoned, starved, grief-stricken, injured, broken, crippled, abused, mentally-challenged, homeless, paralyzed, blind, deaf, numb, neglected, discriminated against, scarred, drained, alone, hopeless, or fearful—or have been ridiculed, threatened, emotionally assaulted, robbed, beaten, intimidated, wrongfully accused, stalked, or bullied—or have suffered from loss, extortion, destruction, wounding, burns, being crushed, sprained or strained—or if you ever had to run away to survive, or worse—God was there. God *is here*. God *will always be* faithful to those who love His Son and to those whom His Son loves. Reach out to Him. He is available.

Can we say the same?

Deuteronomy 7:9-11, 31:6-8 ❧ 2 Corinthians 1:8-10
Hebrews 2:17-18, 10:23 ❧ John 14:1-6
Revelation 21:5-8 ❧ Habakkuk 3:17-19
Psalm 66:5-12, 16-20 ❧ Zephaniah 3:17

THE HEAVINESS OF SIN

Sin changed everything that God designed, taking our world from spiritually flawless and pure, to broken, twisted, and dark. The Lord didn't taint His workmanship; man's choice to spiritually separate from Him was responsible for the moral and physical decline of the world.

When the Bible talks about sin, it often refers to our iniquities leading to death. This isn't saying that our bodies will literally die from sinning, though sinful choices and actions may decrease longevity. The scriptures refer to spiritual death leading to a life that becomes so distant from God that – when the body expires – God allows us to continue our eternal spiritual life in that darkness. Our existence becomes completely apart from Him, inundated by the evil and sin that we wholeheartedly embraced while in human form, but without any of the pleasure we once passionately sought.

Sin is a very heavy burden to carry, especially when it can be alluring and self-gratifying in the short term, only to open wider the abyss of challenges, misery, and emptiness in the long run. The world teaches that sin is the way to find fulfillment and peace, but the opposite is true. The weight of sin preoccupies the mind, weakens the spirit, destroys relationships, is usually accompanied by feelings of guilt, shame, regret, fear and anger, impacts the intellect, influences our perceptions of reality, and many other negative consequences. Only by denying sin can we find wholeness in the Lord.

In His omnipresence, God witnessed mankind's entire history before He created Adam. He saw all the ugliness, perversion, hatred, and forms of evil to come once sin entered the world. Yet,

He set a plan of infinite mercy in motion to give us hope despite our sin. He desired for us to have a relationship with Him beyond our limited organic lifespans. That possibility came solely through Jesus,

If God were to hold us accountable for "settling up" when we die, none of us (no, not one) would stand a chance of escaping an eternity of unimaginable torture. This reality isn't due to our Father's lack of forgiveness but because of His perfect justice without prejudice. We cannot spiritually justify sinning, since He has put an awareness of good and evil/right and wrong in all of us.

Do we feel the heavy burden of responsibility and consequences for our sinful choices? Do these decisions punish our minds, tax our emotions, and burden our bodies with stress? Have we apologized, repented and sought His forgiveness? Or do we honestly believe that we can handle the eternal yoke of sin without divine intervention and have it result in a positive outcome?

Isaiah 59:1-16 ❧ Romans 3:10-26, 7:15-21, 8:10

Acts 5:1-11 ❧ Philippians 3:18-19 ❧ James 1:13-15, 4:17

Galatians 6:7-9 ❧ Mark 9:43-48 ❧ Ezekiel 18:20-28

God's Priorities Versus Man's Materialism

Mankind has put many idols ahead of, or in place of, the Lord. Books could be written about this subject, but my focus will be on the Christian "holidays" that are celebrated in the United States.

When Christ came to sacrifice Himself for the world's sins forever, the Old Testament ritual sacrifices were no longer required, since God had given the only perfect Sacrifice for all time, His Son. Jesus instructed us to put God above everything else in our lives and embrace His holiness and love for His family. When Christ honored His Father, He didn't do it through purchasing gifts for everyone He knew or demanding that people decorate their homes and communities to celebrate. He modeled a God who esteems our time spent with Him, our resources dedicated to doing His will, and that He is the top priority in our lives. We will never be able to give Him anything comparable to what He has done for us. (Note: The Bible does not reference how, if at all, Jesus and his family celebrated His birthday.)

Yet Christians and non-Christians alike have turned days and seasons that should be considered sacred into circuses of materialism. Christmas is a perfect example. This holiday now justifies record spending in the U.S. for the last eight weeks (or more) of each calendar year. Christian holy days, primarily Christmas and Easter, generate ridiculous levels of retail activity by believers and non-believers around the world, and provide expectations of cards, gifts, parties, and other traditions for their families, friends, coworkers, neighbors, and communities. Now, I'm not saying that wanting to love up on and appreciate others is a bad thing. However, if we claim to be celebrating God, shouldn't that time, energy, and money be invested in our relationship with Him? Why do we shower our human companions with gifts during His times of honor instead of showing them our affection during the other eleven months of the year?

The Lord commands that He be our first Love and most intimate relationship, but these spiritual holiday celebrations seem to have done the opposite to many Christians. Our to-do lists, unpacking, and decorating lists (house—indoors and outdoors, yard, car, etc.), gift lists, baking lists, guest lists, visit lists, donation lists, delivery lists, Christmas card lists, and more (just for the month before Christmas), have squeezed the Lord out or pushed Him to the "if-I-have-time" list. For some, the only peace during the season comes either during the quiet of a church service or after everything is done, cleaned up, packed up, thank you notes written/mailed, relatives departed for home, and trash cans taken to the curb.

Generally, Easter is less traumatic for adults, since buying candy, baskets andstuffed animals, attending an Easter egg hunt, and possibly visiting relatives take much less energy and effort than choreographing the multitude of Christmas activities over a handful of weeks.

My point is that we have lost sight of and slighted the birth, death and resurrection of the world's Savior by creating our own form of worship, and it is not of Him. We should be ecstatic and eager to honor Jesus and His Father for their infinite mercy, grace and personal sacrifices, but our holiday rituals demonstrate that we value stuff, symbols, and activities totally unrelated to God and His selflessness toward us. Our intentions may be God-based, but our follow-through and lack of Christ-centered focus distances us from the very Person we claim to embrace and worship. Even nonbelievers use the routine created by Christians to perpetuate an excuse for gift giving, indulgences and vacations, though they have no desire to know the Lord, or experience His love and forgiveness. Ironically, both groups appear to become completely consumed and overwhelmed by their own holiday expectations and commitments instead of Christians using the time to grow closer to the Lord and ministering to "...the least of these...."

Christians will be judged by a different standard, since we have been given the Gospel message and accept it. Not only are we accountable and expected to share His Word with nonbelievers, our words and actions should set us apart. This includes not blending in with the roar of materialism and worship of stuff during holy days.

Many believers do celebrate God in a healthy fashion, keeping a perspective of truth, regarding the Lord above all else and loving others like themselves. They do not lose sight of Him in the distracting clutter of holiday stress. But for most, this is not the case. Can you imagine how God must shake His head when He watches us during seasons that should honor Him? Millions of people with elevated blood pressure, throwing money in every direction, some going into debt to purchase meaningless things, many becoming angry and violent when unable to find or purchase specific items, schedules monopolized with holiday obligations, worship of a man in a red suit who brings children toys (except to those who are poor, homeless or struggling to survive in Third World countries), and total exhaustion, all supposedly to show Him our love and appreciation.

Imagine if our worship took the form of foregoing buying additional luxuries for our family and friends, decorations and miscellaneous excess holiday items, and instead investing our resources in the less fortunate and their needs. What if we didn't flood the internet and retail stores like maniac locusts to devour every possible product? What if we sowed our blessings into the kingdom and used them to lift those for whom we are supposed to be advocating? What if we spent more time listening to God's call for us to seek Him in quiet and stillness, or meeting the needs of the less fortunate, instead of obsessing over our own schedules and the wants of people in our circles of friends?

With most Christian holy days, the chasm between a Lord-centered awareness and the all-consuming-holiday-centric experience is ever increasing. Please give time, thought and prayer to where the Lord stands in the scope of your, and your family's, holiday routines. Is He in the middle of the celebration, basking in your love and gratitude, or is He watching from the sidelines of your life, having been replaced by fictional characters, sweets and presents?

If we truly love the Lord, we don't need a holiday to justify honoring Him. If we truly love others, we don't require a holiday to justify blessing them. If we are truly Christians, our relationship with God shouldn't be dictated by a calendar, nor our gift giving prompted by seasonal sales and commercial ads. Faith should lead us.

Luke 2:4-21 ⚜ Leviticus 23 ⚜ Romans 14:5-9

Jeremiah 10:1-5 ⚜ Mark 7:5-9 ⚜

Philippians 2:5-12 ⚜ Isaiah 55:8-9

SO MUCH MORE

The strength we draw from our Father is more fortified than the average person's self-discipline or simple will power. He equips us with the ability to overcome the hurdles and roadblocks that life provides, though it cannot be rationally explained by nonbelievers. His authority goes far beyond the shallowness of self-help mantras and intellectual approaches to problems.

He has also blessed us with an incomprehensible peace, even amidst intimidating, chaotic and disruptive people, events and circumstances. He offers us a holy retreat under His wings, a quiet, spiritual calm that envelopes us in moments of greatest need as we cry out for help, rest, freedom from our pain, relief from our fear, or escape from our grief.

Also, consider His gift of wisdom that He freely shares in His Word and by placing it in our seeking spirits. The lessons in the books of Proverbs and Psalms, alone, could take lifetimes to fully savor and grasp, and many ideas from these passages have been adopted by the secular world as popular catch phrases and words-to-live-by, even though they fall under a "religious" heading. An amazing quality about the Bible is that, being the inspired Word of God, the world cannot help but see its truth even though it opposes their beliefs and desires. In addition, regardless of how many times they have read it, the Bible speaks to Christians in different ways and provides revelation at different times. No wonder it is called the "Living Word!"

Let's not forget patience, a unique attribute of God and a quality that makes us more like Jesus. As many times as God repeats Himself to us in the Bible, He clearly is the Master of longsuffering. He has made us His army, so we are able to offer the same patience to others time after time. As often as He has dealt with our numerous poor choices, impulses, shortcomings, and sins, He remains faithful and expects us to do likewise with our family, friends, neighbors, and strangers.

The most profound of the Lord's infinite gifts is love. Every element of God's character – His perfection, judgment, compassion, knowledge, might, and creativity – stem from the core of His pure being. He cherishes mankind, despite our waywardness, sin and self-centered nature. Embracing us in spite of these behaviors speaks volumes about His devotion to His family, as do the measures He was willing to take to save us from eternal damnation. We can do nothing for Him, yet He loves us anyway, without a hidden agenda or manipulation. He loved us first, so that we would know how to love each other.

If we are followers of Jesus, consider how much un-repayable, undeserved and unearned generosity the Trinity has shown us. The persons of God are much more than you think they are, as are the many divine treasures, skills, and blessings we have had bestowed upon us as holy servants. Are you treating Them with the respect, honor, and gratitude of which they are worthy?

1 Corinthians 12:4-12 ❧ James 1:4-5

Exodus 28:2-4, 31:1-11 ❧ 2 Peter 3:8-9

Acts 2:1-6 ❧ Galatians 5:22-25

The "I" Obsession

Once upon a time, a friend invited me to his wedding. By request from the bride and groom, disposable cameras had been placed on the reception tables for guests to use to take pictures of the event. Ideally, this would include as many details of the celebration as possible: the guests, decorations, significant special moments, and other details. A couple at my table enthusiastically exhausted the entire roll of film—on themselves! Now keep in mind that this was back twenty-plus years ago, before smart phones. I was shocked at their level of narcissism and vanity, especially when someone else was paying to have the film developed! I could already imagine the bride and groom sitting down to enjoy these special wedding memories and getting to that particular batch of photos. I heard their scoffs and saw their eyes roll. Little did I know that it was a glimpse of what was to come only a few years into the future.

As I set pen to paper, we now have more physical and digital tools available for self-glorification than ever before. As a society and across the globe, the time we spend absorbed with ourselves, as individuals, has become totally ridiculous and quite scary. We have become a culture of "selfie" worship! Obviously, this is not an accurate description of everyone, but it certainly holds true for the majority. Sadly, many people claiming to be Christians are part of this "I"—obsessed culture.

Our plethora of phones, tablets, laptops, watches, TVs, and other electronic devices enable us to have the instant gratification of photographing of ourselves to put on display to family, friends or anyone with an internet connection. Facebook, Twitter, Instagram, Tick Tok, and YouTube are only a few of the variety of social media memberships available to encourage people to share all their personal life details and opinions with the world. We have become so self-revolving (and equipping generations of youth to be parented and entertained by electronics) that I have seen whole families at restaurants completely consumed by their phones. The only conversation was with the server to place drink and food orders! The U.S. and other countries around the world have provided citizens with means by which to disconnect from the idea of genuine communication (talking in person), individuals sharing quality time together, and strengthening relationships by everyday life activities not based on technology.

At some point over the last thirty years, a significant number of parents across multiple generations opted to become their kids' friends instead of their parents. Now we have multiple generations who embrace the lie that life is all about them and how the world is expected to cater to their wants. They have been taught to believe (and had this reinforced by the media) that the world revolves around them. Parents believe that cell phones and other entertainment should be provided to their children at an early age, and children believe that they are entitled to whatever whim they desire. These parents continue to reinforce and perpetuate this fallacy and have created generations of youngsters who behave as victims when they do not have their demands met.

The majority of our society is no longer about the team but instead about the emotions and opinions of the self—the "I" which will not hear or except whatever the "I" deems to be uncomfortable, inconvenient, not interesting, un-gratifying or some other shallow premise. People are failing to think for themselves, losing discernment between reality and fiction, and are letting their emotions destroy their common sense and impulse control.

As Christians, we need to hold ourselves accountable to being part of the solution by gaining control over this slow-motion train wreck in our own lives. Our affirmation comes from the Lord, not from the number of followers we have, who likes our posts, or whatever witty comments we can launch into cyberspace. Seriously? Twenty to thirty years ago, families still had meals together, at a single table, with conversations about real life where listening and questions were commonplace. Family interactions included discussions about conflict and consequences for misbehavior that involved actual punishment. Kids' extracurricular activities and sports generated a winning team and a losing team. We did not protect children from the reality of losing (to protect the "I") and instead reassured them that it was okay not to win every competition. These simple cause-and-effect events help build character by allowing children to experience the ups and downs of life without having them judged as personal flaws or failures. They learned about conflict resolution, problem solving and developing in-person communication skills versus the option of denying reality by tuning the world out and tuning in to their choice of tech.

A significant number of basic elements are missing in kids' maturation today, because they are spending more time in the "I" presence instead of the "We" team (both God and family). The mealtime example perfectly illustrates the importance of human interaction. Back in the day, nothing electronic ran in the house during meals or homework time, unless it was for subtle background music or being used for meal purposes, so we could focus on and be present with each other. We were *engaged* in living within communities at home, work or school and in social circles. These days, you are considered fortunate if you are able to speak (in person) with someone who gives you direct eye contact, is not already suffering from permanent neck damage (from looking down at their phone), hasn't completely succumbed to carpel tunnel syndrome (from texting) and who doesn't twitch or panic every 37 seconds if they haven't checked their phones. How are we supposed to strengthen the faith of our families and others when we lack control over these "I" dynamics?

My brothers and sisters in Christ, please understand that I share this in love. These "I" obsessions have become idols that we have come to worship in plain sight. We allow them to control our behavior, distract us through ego stroking and fear, and distance us from God by pre-occupying our thoughts and perverting our priorities. We must stop making excuses and trying to justify why they must be incorporated into or present every moment of our day.

Please take authority over your mindsets and these tools; put them in appropriate perspective. They are useful, but are they necessarily good? If they are consuming most of one's time and attention, where does that leave a genuine relationship with the Lord, family, friends, coworkers, neighbors, church members, and others? Consider the quality of what you would want those relationships to be had smart phones or the internet never been invented. Tech is not a surrogate—nor should it ever be an excuse—to ignore God, loved ones or anyone else. You have control, so please exercise it in a manner that honors the only One who is worthy! The only "I" obsession we should have is for Immanuel!

1 Corinthians 10:23-24 ✤ Psalm 135:15-18

Mark 12:28-34 ✤ Deuteronomy 4:23-40

2 Timothy 3:1-5 ✤ Jonah 2:8 ✤ Isaiah 44:6-20

YOUR DISCOMFORT ZONE

My faith has seen me through all sorts of challenges over many years. God has been extremely generous with His companionship, forgiveness, protection, and provision in my life. He has blessed me with supportive relatives and friends in His kingdom family as well as carried me through injuries, divorce, job loss, and other painful realities. As much as I savor the seasons of peace, celebration and restoration that His favor gives me, I know that He does His most profound work within me when I feel surrounded and overwhelmed by uncomfortable circumstances.

These high walls, steep drops and dark recesses in my journey are the times when I cling determinedly to His hand, because their perspectives acutely remind me of how inadequate my efforts alone are in this world. I can do nothing of true value without Him. Yet, even with His infinite power and wisdom, He allows me to choose our time together, my availability to serve Him and my neighbors, and to what degree I desire to pursue a richer relationship.

Regardless of how much time I spend with the Lord, real life drama continues to knock on my door. If we genuinely seek Him, we will find ourselves in uncomfortable—and often painful—situations that require a firm faith footing before moving forward. It's okay to squirm, weep, cry out, question, or react in other ways, so long as those emotions and responses do not weaken our grasp of our Father's hand. He will never let go; but He permits us to break contact and distance ourselves. Do not get drawn into a self-pity party that lasts indefinitely. Do not allow anger, fear or grief to drive a wedge into our holy intimacy with God. Do not let our insecurities lead us to the pseudo-comfort of "Christian" tale spinners with promises of healing and guidance through channels apart from the Lord. Fervently guard and value our faith, since it is the core from which the rest of us grows.

Embrace being uncomfortable but continue to be aware of His love enveloping us while He transforms us into people more like His Son. Relish His stretching of our souls to better fit His purpose for our lives. Meditate upon the truth that His deep care for us includes answering every prayer and treasuring every conversation. Understand that His thoughts and ways are higher than ours and are focused on what is most beneficial for us, both now and in the context of forever.

Be awake, alert and attentive to the hard times, as their lessons are far deeper, higher and wider than they appear to be. Consider them endurance training and preparation for finishing the race, when we will experience the joy of having fought the good fight to victory in Christ, never to be uncomfortable again.

Romans 5:3-4, 8:18 ❧ 2 Corinthians 4:8-18

Psalm 55:22 ❧ 1 Peter 4:12-19

2 Corinthians 1:3-7 ❧ Revelation 21:1-4

POWERFUL JOURNEYS—
ARE YOU PAYING ATTENTION?

Speaking strictly as someone without a theology degree or formal training in Christianity, I think that God created His Word to cater to humans with limited intellects (compared to His)—but with deep potential—as spiritual beings. Even though the Bible is extremely brief compared to the immeasurable existence of the Lord, its words contain amazing power and revelation for those whose hearts belong to Him.

When I consider what He chose to include within the cover of His book, the largest portion appears to be lessons about who He is, how to draw closer to Him, how to live healthier lives, how to effectively support others, and stories about people whose journeys and testimonies played profound roles in history as members of God's family.

However, as His followers, are we truly honoring these teachings? For instance, the famous King David—a "man after God's own heart"—was guilty of adultery, having a man murdered, and getting a married woman pregnant through his uncontained lust, poor decisions, and lack of self-control. Although some believe that she intentionally bathed where he could see her, his reactions to the situation were his responsibility, both as a king and a man. The Lord first admonished him by sending Nathan to confront him about taking something that was not his, then God killed David's young son. David humbled himself before the Lord and repented of his sins, taking full ownership of his behavior and the consequences for them. The Lord showed him mercy and favor because He saw David's heart of faith and trust in Him, not through scorekeeping to compare good choices versus bad or what David thought he'd earned or deserved. If that was the case, David would not have received God's forgiveness by anyone's standard.

Today, many people, whether in leadership positions or not, claim to be Christians but lack the accountability, humility and repentance that David displayed in his relationship with God, even if these behaviors were not immediately apparent. Like David, we can also know the joy and grace God pours out on us when we repent for our sins. However, for those people who are not sincerely sorry for their sins, nor interested in getting to the matters of the heart, they will remain in bondage, pain and unfulfillment. Their "faith" does not align with God's instruction and His offer of forgiveness and grace.

Another significant model of faith is Job. Had the Lord chosen to leave Job's history out of the Bible, we wouldn't know about his struggle through unimaginable pain and suffering. Millions of people over thousands of years would have been denied reading the account of his experience and perseverance through unbelievable trauma and loss. He was someone who would rather have died than continue with the misery of what his life had become. The death of his ten children at the same time, the destruction of his property and livestock, and the infliction of personal physical illness and torment were the most horrific ways that the devil could try to drive a wedge between Job and God. He was hoping to cause Job to blaspheme and hate the Lord. But Job—as grief-stricken and abandoned as he felt—refused to curse God. The Book of Job ends with a lengthy response from the Lord to Job and his misguided friends, reminding them of who He is and who they are not. The final picture we are given of Job's life includes God's restoration of his family (ten children), his property (an increase of livestock), and longevity enough to have time to get know his new family to multiple generations. Although God did not spare Job from the pain of his experiences, He did heal and prosper him for his faithfulness.

Job's character is phenomenal! His story is a crucial reminder that clinging to our faith is essential, no matter what we are surviving. We can expect trials throughout our lives because we live in a broken world, and the devil never stops trying to destroy believers' relationships with their Creator. Even people who aren't Christians know the history of Job, so his suffering wasn't an effort in futility. He taught us what is possible and gave all credit for his blessings right back to God.

Each of us has personal experiences and family, friends or acquaintances who are carrying—or have carried—heavy, tragic burdens that have no logical reason behind them. A world impacted by sin opens the door for unexplainable suffering. We cannot rationalize why such things happen, but we do have control over how these chaotic events impact our relationship with our heavenly Father. It IS within our control to move through our circumstances while leaning on Him, crying in His presence, sharing our anger and frustration, and praying for His mercy and healing. He is always with us.

But these hard times may encourage some "Christians" to step away from God, whether by claiming that He is responsible for our misery or by endorsing others' theories and explanations that are not scripturally sound. God should be in the center of our reactions to pain—not pushed to the side or disregarded due to our desire to know why things happen or our hope and expectation of divine intervention. The Lord's apparent inaction is not an indication of the absence of His love, concern, or compassion. He is always moving on behalf of His family, praying and singing over us and counting our tears.

I enjoy the many accounts of faithful followers in the Bible and how God uses their challenges to fulfill His will. We are given descriptions of each person's struggles and decisions for a reason, and it may be to help us gain perspective regarding our own journeys with the Lord. The circumstances of the people who had major roles in scripture, whether good or evil, reveal various aspects of God's nature and His perfect plan. Without Pharaoh's refusal to free the Israelites, the Egyptians would not have understood that God's wrath was an intentional and clear consequence of Pharaoh's rejection of Moses' demands on God's behalf. At the same time, the Israelites experienced God's protection and favor, witnessing the fulfillment of the prophecies from their own history! And so it was for the multitude of those, believers and non-believers alike, who came before us as witnesses providing a framework for strengthening our faith: Abraham, Noah, Esther, Balaam, the Apostles, the judges and kings, Abigail, Nebuchadnezzar, Samuel, Ruth, and Pontius Pilate, to name a few.

None of their lives were ideal, even those to whom God spoke directly, and most encountered obstacles I am sure they would have preferred to avoid. But God's people served His purposes to the best of their ability and gave us glimpses of His love, devotion, and eagerness to advocate for His family. Even the nonbelievers played key roles in illustrating parts of His plan and demonstration of His power.

The Lord has offered us the holy opportunity to be His children—more than simply His biologic creation—His spiritual family for eternity. Are you taking advantage of His sacred invitation and letting it transform your character and heart into ones the Lord can use? Are you embracing His desire for obedience, humility and a repentant spirit? Are you willing to cling to Him, no matter what your circumstances? Have you offered Him your life for His kingdom?

2 Samuel 11, 12:1-14 ⚭ Numbers 22 & 23

Book of Job ⚭ Book of Ruth ⚭ Genesis 6-9:17

CHRISTIANITY IS NOT A BUFFET OF DOCTRINES

The number of "religions" recognized worldwide is mind boggling. Some have adopted philosophies and ideals from historic figures while others are newer and have been shaped based on political, oppositional or purely fictional points of view. Yet none of them demonstrates the vast compassion, sacrifice, and love that the Lord showed mankind through the life and death of Jesus. Family members of Christ need to be careful not to casually accept untrue, manmade doctrines or blend false teachings into the Word of God. *Popularity does not define or confirm fact.* Historically, the morals, values, and concepts that Jesus taught were resented by the "educated" religious leaders of His days on Earth. However, many commoners yearned for the freedom He offered through the forgiveness of sin.

There are a lot of belief systems labeled as "faith" by modern-day institutions and cultures around the globe. Any list could not possibly be exhaustive, but many appear to mimic the relationship hierarchy, commandments, and teachings of the Lord and His Christ. This is no coincidence. Remember that the devil's most powerful tool is his lie, and the most effective lies are the ones that are *partial* truths.

For instance, some "faiths" have figureheads that are similar to Yahweh or the Trinity, though their names and the roles they have or responsibilities they possess are different. Others are focused on worshipping creation itself, whether specific people, animals, plants, stars and planets, meteorological events or all of the above. For many individuals, their worship is centered on self or people in general (including family members, friends, organization-based relationships, etc.). They adhere to the belief that the world revolves around and is controlled by man, not the Creator. Some bow down to the universe in its entirety, and others believe in reincarnation. The menu of unfulfilling, sinful choices is endless!

In addition to the narratives that ancient and modern cultures have designed to explain away the true God, the allure of power, wealth, fame, and lust and the fulfillment they promise draws a significant number of people away from following the Lord. Jobs, hobbies and forms of entertainment can become all-consuming distractions and primary investments of our time and energy, encouraging a form of empty worship whether we intend them to be or not. Our technology has become a god for many, and those who are addicted are quick to justify exactly why it is essential for them to be "connected" at all times. Emotions also have a large, dedicated audience of people who have become so focused on their feelings, whether with seemingly healthy qualities (love, devotion) or lack of control over negative influences (anger, fear, hatred), that the emotions monopolize their time and skew their perceptions of reality. A significant segment of the population has become pre-occupied with appearances, and some individuals have become obsessed with maintaining the illusion of beauty, status and other characteristics they believe meet with society's approval. Then, there are students of science and knowledge who spend their lives trying to disprove the existence of God, thereby worshipping whatever truth they have created in their own eyes.

Even believers with good intentions frequently wander from the narrow path, whether in thought or deed, often over time and in small steps that subtly decrease our interest in faith and increase our concern for everything else.

Regardless of the focus, anything that becomes more important than one's faith is considered to be a false god because it draws our attention and energy away from our relationship with our Maker.

As you can imagine, all ideas and worship practices are fair game within the realm of mankind's attempts to seek spiritual enlightenment and to rationalize who we are, why we are here, and how we should live. We have also been inundated with false gods within our everyday lives, from people to emotions to science to battling our insecurities. The saddest part of bearing witness to these pre-occupations and faulty belief systems is that Christians understand that these paths lead to death and a horrible, painful existence in eternal isolation from God.

Do you make a conscious effort to prevent incorporating other beliefs into your understanding of Christianity? Are you policing your thoughts and behaviors regarding where you invest your time and attention to prevent worshipping anything other than the Lord? Do you challenge your fellow Christians whose words, actions and attitudes do not align with scripture?

Are you praying for people who follow other doctrines? Are you trying to share the Gospel message with them? Are you prepared to answer their questions about Jesus? What are you doing to act as an intercessor for those who don't share the eyes and ears that the Lord has given you to experience His love and grace? Are you asking for His mercy while reflecting His light for them to see? Do you genuinely want others to share in the salvation Jesus so freely provided mankind? If not, why not?

2 Timothy 4:1-4 ❧ Galatians 1:6-12

Romans 16:17-19 ❧ 2 Peter 2:1-22

Deuteronomy 18:18-22 ❧ 1 Samuel 5–6:16

WARNINGS

The Bible is full of warnings from God: Warnings to help guide and protect us from ourselves, from others, and from painful eternal consequences.

Do not take these casually, selectively, or deflect the messages; God does not lie, and He does not change. The Lord used His Word to make sure we understood why, how, when, where, and who we are in relationship to our Father. He shares with us His plans for those who love Him, descriptions of heaven for His family, and consistent reminders of the hell (absence of God) that awaits nonbelievers and lukewarm Christians after their physical bodies die.

The Lord leaves no room for confusion using the scriptures' warnings or references to the suffering awaiting unrepentant sinners, unless it is in man's "interpretation" of said verses. Perhaps people try to rewrite these passages to comfort themselves rather than face the reality of their sin and their helplessness and inability to gain salvation on their own.

Regardless of how capable *we* think we are, none of us can escape the perfect judgment to come. Negotiating is not an option. Strength, power, fame and fortune are irrelevant. Reputation, good works, generosity and beauty have no authority before God. The only way to enter through the pearly gates is by God's grace and love in the form of His Son. Our faith and repentance will usher our souls homeward. Since Jesus knows our intent, we cannot manipulate His perception or the results of His final decision over our lifetime of words, choices, and actions. They are all filtered through the truth of our hearts and Christ's relationship with us. If that relationship is superficial on our end, we will be cast out from the Lord's presence forever.

If you have any doubts about the seriousness of His final decree, please read the next few excerpts as a reminder of promises that the Lord will keep at the end of this age.

~But we know that the judgment of God is according to truth against those who practice such things. And do you think this, O man, you who judge those practicing such things and doing the same, that you will escape the judgment of God? Or do you despise the riches of His goodness, forbearance, and longsuffering, not knowing that the goodness of God leads you to repentance? But in accordance with your hardness and your impenitent heart you are treasuring up for yourself wrath in the day of wrath and revelation of the righteous judgment of God, who 'will render to each one according to his deeds': eternal life to those who by patient continuance in doing good seek for glory, honor and immortality; but to those who are self-seeking and do not obey the truth but obey unrighteousness—indignation and wrath, tribulation and anguish, on every soul of man who does evil, of the Jew first and also of the Greek; but glory, honor and peace to everyone who works what is good, to the Jew first and also to the Greek. For there is no partiality with God. Romans 2:2-11

~For the wages of sin is death, but the gift of God is eternal life in Christ Jesus our Lord. Romans 6:23

*~**Enter by the narrow gate; for wide is the gate and broad is the way that leads to destruction, and there are many who go in by it. Because narrow is the gate and difficult is the way which leads to life, and there are few who find it.*** Matthew 7:13-14

*~**And being in torments in Hades, he lifted his eyes and saw Abraham afar off and Lazarus in his bosom. The he cried and said, 'Father Abraham, have mercy on me, and send Lazarus that he may dip the tip of his finger in water and cool my tongue; for I am tormented in this flame.' But Abraham said, 'Son,***

remember that in your lifetime you received your good things, and likewise Lazarus evil things; but now he is comforted, and you are tormented.' Luke 16:23-25

~And do not fear those who kill the body but cannot kill the soul. But rather fear Him who is able to destroy both soul and body in hell. Matthew 10:28

Be diligent in pursuing your faith, lest you become complacent and begin to take Jesus' sacrifice for granted. Take heed of His warnings rooted in love and compassion and remember the Father's plan "…that the world through Him might be saved." We are all part of the "might" until Jesus decides where our new, final home will be.

A Few Thoughts for the Road

We can try to express to the world how amazing Jesus is. Better than explaining Him to others, we need to show them by exemplifying His goodness. We must let His passion and fire burn in our beings so that there is no doubt as to Whom we belong. That being said, sin is an ever-present saboteur waiting for an opportunity to undercut our spiritual journey with God and foil our attempts to spread the Gospel message.

Charles Spurgeon was a man of faith from the 1800's who, I feel, was a gifted teacher and had a way with words. I have included two excerpts for your consideration from his sermons regarding sin and its consequences below:

As the salt flavors every drop in the Atlantic, so does sin affect every atom of our nature. It is so sadly there, so abundantly there, that if you cannot detect it, you are deceived. (C.H. Spurgeon, *Honest Dealing with God*, 1875)

There is an essential difference between the decease of the godly and the death of the ungodly. Death comes to the ungodly man as a penal infliction, but to the righteous as a summons to his Father's palace. To the sinner it is an execution, to the saint an undressing from his sins and infirmities. Death to the wicked is the King of terrors. Death to the saint is the end of terrors, the commencement of glory. (C.H. Spurgeon, *Though He Were Dead*, 1884)

Many Christians are currently convinced that they are "saved" but are living in a manner that begs the question as to whether they actually believe in God. They exude sinful conduct—which is contrary to our Lord's teachings—perpetuating hatred, malice, anger, abuse, and fear, yet insisting their behavior is acceptable. These disillusioned souls are adrift and moving further away from their salvation each day. Sooner than we think, it will be too late to change the gate through which we will pass for eternity.

A few things to ponder as you finish this book and set it aside:

~We are not the ones who define sin; God is. He does not accept our rationale for justifying sin, our reasoning as to which sins are better or worse than others, or our desire to embrace and enjoy sinning.

~We are ALL sinners. We will ALL fail. We ALL need Jesus and the salvation His death provided. Period.

~Do we have a *genuine* relationship with Him?

~Are we asking Him what we need to do for Him, or are we telling Him what He should be doing for us?

~Do we demand more and more from Him versus spending time in His presence humbly apologizing for our sins and thanking Him for our blessings?

~Are we more wrapped up in what others think of us rather than what He thinks of us?

~Are we taking ownership of our faith or living in an undisciplined and self-gratifying reality?

~Are we seeking the Lord's will for our lives or expecting Him to fall in line with ours?

~Do we understand that our ongoing dedication to Jesus (now and moving forward) will determine whether He will advocate for us to be with Him forever?

~If our physical lives were to end today with our professing to love and serve God, are we confident that He will agree with us when judgment is delivered?

I hope you have found a nugget or two of wisdom in this work, since all I can aspire to do is pass along messages that have been given to me. I pray that it has in some way strengthened your faith.

God's teachings and expectations are clear, and perhaps these pages have provided an opportunity for you to think about your relationship with Him. Please seriously examine your priorities when it comes to how you feel about Jesus and contemplate how you treat Him. How would He describe the time you spend together? What are *you* willing to invest in your relationship?

He has already given Everything.

NOTES

Basic Biblical Christian Beliefs

(All followers of Jesus Christ, regardless of their denomination, should share these beliefs.)

1. God (the Father), Jesus Christ (His Son) and the Holy Spirit existed before, during and after our world was created. (They are sometimes referred to collectively as "God," "Lord," "the Trinity" or "the Godhead.")

2. God is all-powerful (omnipotent), all-knowing (omniscient) and exists in all times at once (omnipresent). He is perfect, without sin, never lies and has no faults.

3. God created all things (seen and unseen) which were good, pure and holy.

4. God gives man the ability to be aware of Him, to be in a relationship with Him, and the opportunity to receive the salvation required to live on with Him in heaven, after man's earthly death. In addition to His amazing love, compassion, inspiration, patience, provision, and many other gifts, God gives man free will to choose good or evil.

5. When Adam and Eve disobeyed God by sinning, they were immediately banished from the perfection of God's presence in the Garden of Eden. God explained to them the difficulties and pain they would experience because of their sin (behavior that separated them from Him), and He told them that their world would no longer be as it had in the Garden. The world would be impacted by the sin introduced through their disobedience, that forced them outside of God's home. They would know suffering through the lens of a fallen and broken world that is no longer spiritually pure.

6. Before Christ, God gave His chosen people, the Jewish people of the nation of Israel, rules about behavior, consequences, required sacrifices for atonement, mandatory feast days, and other guidelines by which they were to live. These instructions were for their own spiritual and physical well-being and to keep them from distancing themselves from the Lord.

7. God's Ten Commandments carved by Him on stone tablets in the presence of Moses to be followed by the Israelites and Christians by adoption:

> I. I am the Lord your God, who brought you out of the land of Egypt, out of the house of bondage. You shall have no other gods before Me.
>
> II. You shall not make for yourself a carved image – any likeness of anything that is in heaven above, or that is in the earth beneath, or that is in the water under the earth; you shall not bow down to them nor serve them.
>
> III. You shall not take the name of the Lord in vain, for the Lord will not hold him guiltless who takes His name in vain.
>
> IV. Remember the Sabbath day, to keep it holy.
>
> V. Honor your father and your mother, that your days may be long upon the land which the Lord your God is giving you.
>
> VI. You shall not murder.
>
> VII. You shall not commit adultery.
>
> VIII. You shall not steal.
>
> IX. You shall not bear false witness against your neighbor.

X. You shall not covet your neighbor's house; you shall not covet your neighbor's wife, nor his male servant, nor his female servant, nor his ox, nor his donkey, nor anything that is your neighbor's.

8. When Jesus came into the world, He helped man learn more about the Father through His actions, lessons and miracles. Where the Old Covenant that the Lord had with His chosen people had been broken, God sent His Son to bring a New Covenant to cover all mankind. This sacred relationship with the Father was now open both to the Jewish people and to nonbelievers (Gentiles), whether they came to follow Christ or not.

9. Where Adam was one man who brought sin into the world, the Son of God was the perfect and blameless Sacrifice required to forgive and pay the debt of sin for all people for all time. Since Jesus' life was the propitiation for all sins of every soul to ever exist (not just believers), no more sacrifices were required for sin. His suffering and death gave every man the opportunity to have eternal life.

10. Jesus' ultimate sacrifice does not guarantee salvation for those who do not believe in Him and repent of their sins. He has given the world the opportunity to be saved by grace, and no one comes to the Father except through Him. He is the Way, the Truth, and the Life.

11. Jesus Christ (Yeshua) is the only person who fulfills hundreds of Old Testament prophecies of the Messiah…going back through thousands of years of history…including His birthplace, travels, teaching, miracle-working, arrest, torture, death and resurrection. Thousands of people experienced or witnessed His healings and instruction, and over five hundred people saw Him after He was raised from the dead. No other person has or

will fulfill these prophecies. Jesus is the only Savior, the only Salvation.

12. The Bible is the inspired Word of God. The forty authors of the sixty-six books did not write of or by themselves, but by the working of the Holy Spirit within them. Only Divine guidance could share future events, people, places, and insight with these writers and coordinate the accuracy and continuity of the many texts over thousands of years and a multitude of generations.

13. The history of the Bible was experienced by thousands of people and recorded by individuals who were faithful followers, some of whom followed the Lord's pillar of smoke by day and pillar of fire by night (the Israelites), or who spoke directly with the Lord in the Old Testament, or who lived with him from His birth through His two-to-three years of ministry at the end of His mortal life. There is no single person, single opinion, or single account of the revelation of Christ, His lineage, His ability to heal, His control of nature, or His speaking of knowledge and wisdom beyond our own. His entire life was witnessed by believers and non-believers alike and confirmed to stand alone by other religious leaders/belief systems who could not explain His power and authority, when juxtaposed next to their own faith rationale.

14. God values qualities that the world deems to be weak or unimportant and condemns qualities that the world esteems and glorifies. The spiritual and carnal worlds stand in direct opposition to each other. You cannot faithfully serve God while obsessing over the people and trappings of the world.

15. No number of prayers, sacrifices, donations, hours spent volunteering, religious rituals, amount of income, power, good deeds, friends, speaking to "spiritual people," or following anyone other than Jesus can save you from your sins. Period.

16. God is clear about warning us not to change or pervert His Word or its teachings. We do not have the authority to rewrite the Lord's text, and those that do—to suit their own selfish purposes—will suffer His wrath. God offers salvation forever through His Son in His heavenly home or an eternity in hell. Those who have chased after earthly enticements and reveled in their sin through self-centered endeavors will forever exist in the excruciating anguish of a spiritual dungeon, so-to-speak, completely void of God's presence. The soul lives forever; it's just a matter of where.

17. God states that He will show no partiality when it comes to holding every person accountable for his/her lifetime of thoughts, words and actions. His judgment is perfect, and He considers everyone's history, intentions of the heart and faith in His Son when determining our new eternal homes. He also says that many will cry out Jesus' name and will be told "I never knew you," indicating there will be believers who think that they have salvation, and they won't find out until it is too late that they do not. We have been warned and cannot claim ignorance when Jesus returns to judge the world.

BIBLIOGRAPHY

Spurgeon, C. H. (1875, June 20). *Honest Dealing with God*. Retrieved from https://archive.spurgeon.org/sermons/1241.php

Spurgeon, C. H. (1884, Sept 14). *Though He Were Dead*. Retrieved from https://archive.spurgeon.org/sermons/1799.php

149

Printed in the USA
CPSIA information can be obtained
at www.ICGtesting.com
JSHW041913030823
45860JS00006B/35

9 781628 802610